CAE
Practice Tests 1

TEACHER'S BOOK

Patricia Aspinall
Louise Hashemi

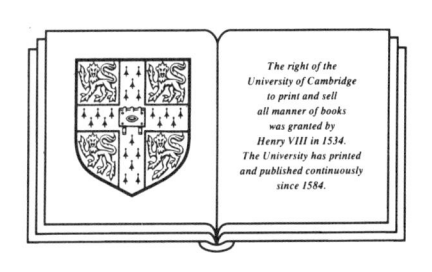

Cambridge University Press
Cambridge
New York   Port Chester
Melbourne   Sydney

Published by the Press Syndicate of the University of Cambridge
The Pitt Building, Trumpington Street, Cambridge CB2 1RP
40 West 20th Street, New York, NY 10011–4211, USA
10 Stamford Road, Oakleigh, Victoria 3166, Australia

© Cambridge University Press 1991

First published 1991

Printed in Great Britain
by Scotprint Ltd, Musselburgh, Scotland

ISBN 0 521 42274 4 Teacher's Book
ISBN 0 521 42276 0 Student's Book
ISBN 0 521 42275 2 Cassettes

Copyright
The law allows a reader to make a single copy of part of a book
for purposes of private study. It does not allow the copying of
entire books or the making of multiple copies of extracts. Written
permission for any such copying must always be obtained from the
publisher in advance.

Contents

Introduction 1

Question aims and formats 3

Marking and grading 8
Assessment and marking of Paper 2 Writing 9
Assessment and marking of Paper 5 Speaking 16

Preparing students for CAE 18

Practice Test 1 22
Paper 1   Reading 22
Paper 2   Writing 22
Paper 3   English in Use 22
Paper 4   Listening 24
Paper 5   Speaking 29

Practice Test 2 32
Paper 1   Reading 32
Paper 2   Writing 32
Paper 3   English in Use 32
Paper 4   Listening 34
Paper 5   Speaking 39

Practice Test 3 42
Paper 1   Reading 42
Paper 2   Writing 42
Paper 3   English in Use 42
Paper 4   Listening 44
Paper 5   Speaking 48

Practice Test 4 51
Paper 1   Reading 51
Paper 2   Writing 51
Paper 3   English in Use 51
Paper 4   Listening 53
Paper 5   Speaking 58

Acknowledgements

The assessment criteria on pp. 15 and 17 and the sample answer sheets in the Student's Book are reproduced by kind permission of the University of Cambridge Local Examinations Syndicate.

Introduction

What is the CAE?

The Certificate in Advanced English (CAE) is an examination in general English introduced by the University of Cambridge Local Examinations Syndicate (UCLES) in 1991. This set of four complete practice tests is aimed to give students help in developing the skills needed to attempt the CAE examination. The examination fits in the range of examinations from elementary level (the Preliminary English Test) through intermediate level (the First Certificate in English) to proficiency standard (the Certificate of Proficiency in English). It is intended to offer students a high-level qualification in the language, which for many will be a significant final achievement, or to prepare them for the more academically demanding CPE.

Level

The level of English reflected in these practice tests, as in the examination, assumes that the student will have passed First Certificate or has achieved a similar standard to a C grade in the FCE. The content of the test materials is chosen to encourage the students to practise the skills which they will need in their jobs and careers, so the practice tests lay stress on real world tasks wherever this is appropriate. For those students who want to continue their study of the language and take the CPE, the tests offer a level of lexis and structure aimed at developing the linguistic skills they will need for this higher level examination.

As in the actual examination, the language level of the instructions, the texts and the individual questions of these practice tests fall within a range from that of First Certificate to a level about two-thirds of the way towards the CPE.

Authentic texts

Most of the texts used in the examination come from authentic sources and the practice tests reflect both this and the resulting increase in language level of the stimulus material. However, care has been taken not to test lexis or structure which falls outside the level unless there are enough clues in the texts to help the students. The amount of material used in this way is similar to that in the actual examination. The texts have been chosen from a wide range of authentic sources – in-flight magazines, newspapers and periodicals, information leaflets and brochures – in order to encourage teachers and students to become accustomed to using 'real' English in the classroom. We hope that the materials are interesting and stimulating for teacher and student alike.

Introduction

Tradition and innovation

Although the examination is similar in format to the FCE and CPE examinations, we believe that the CAE breaks new ground within a traditional framework. The CAE includes some of the latest techniques in language testing and has kept a firm hold on the need for good washback effect on teaching. Similarly, these practice tests aim to give teachers the opportunity to prepare students creatively for the examination. The emphasis on text variety and novel question types, such as the multiple-matching, underlies this aim. At the same time, teachers who are familiar with the FCE and CPE will feel comfortable with the five-paper structure covering the skills of reading, writing, listening and speaking and will recognise the need for the testing of underlying structural competence in the English in Use paper. We hope that teachers will find that these practice tests fit easily into their teaching programmes, develop rather than depress their classroom practice and make examination preparation a more satisfying and enjoyable activity.

The structure of CAE

The examination is divided into five paper components, each of which carries 20 per cent of the total marks. The papers are as follows:

Paper 1	Reading	1 hour
Paper 2	Writing	2 hours
Paper 3	English in Use	1 hour 30 minutes
Paper 4	Listening	45 minutes
Paper 5	Speaking	15 minutes

Question aims and formats

Paper 1 *Reading*

The Reading paper consists of four authentic texts drawn from a range of British and international publications. The texts are laid out, as far as possible, in their original form and are unedited except for original errors. Some texts have been shortened in order to adhere to the word limit imposed by the specification (3,000 words for Paper 1). Texts are sometimes made up from a series of shorter pieces.

There is a wide variety of text types, such as material from leaflets, newspapers and magazines. Plans, diagrams and other types of visuals are used and occasionally include abbreviations or note form when appropriate.

Teachers may feel that 3,000 words is a heavy reading load for students in an examination but the intention is to encourage students to develop different reading skills appropriate to the text and task. In particular, students should practise the skills of skimming and scanning texts for overall impression or specific information. These are real-world skills which the examination and these practice texts hope to develop.

More traditional reading skills (also exemplified in the CPE), such as interpreting the text for inference, attitude and style or deducing meaning from context are also a significant aim of the Reading paper.

The questions are various types of multiple choice, cloze or matching. There may be up to 50 questions in each test, normally carrying one mark each. The raw total is weighted so that it contributes 20 per cent to the total examination mark.

Sometimes the questions are printed before the text in order to show the students that they will need to scan the text for specific information. In this sort of task the student should expect to find that the questions do not necessarily follow the order of the text.

In other parts of the Reading paper the questions follow the text in the normal way and usually the questions follow the order of the text. Those questions which attempt to discover if the student understands the gist or overall impression of a text tend to come towards the end of a series of questions. In some cases more than one set of questions accompanies a text. It is part of the rationale for the CAE that question type, text layout and ordering of questions should reflect the natural aspects of reading competence.

Because this paper is marked by computer, the students are asked to record their answers in the form of letters of the alphabet on an optically marked sheet (OMR). This requires the student to pencil in a lozenge on a single sheet of A4 OMR, as in the reading component of FCE and CPE. It is important that the students use soft pencil as the OMR reader is not sensitive to pen or biro. If a

Question aims and formats

mistake is made, the student should carefully erase the mark with a rubber. Tipp-Ex should not be used.

As the paper is only 60 minutes long, it is probably not a good idea for students to transfer their answers to the OMR sheet at the end of the test. Of course, a record of their marks can still be kept on the question paper, especially if the teacher wants to go over the paper in class at a later stage.

When using these practice tests, students may want to record their answers in the book or on a separate sheet of paper. One sample OMR sheet for Paper 1 is provided at the back of the Student's Book.

Paper 2 Writing

The Writing paper is divided into two sections carrying equal marks. In both Section A and Section B students are asked to do tasks based on materials drawn from a variety of sources including articles, notes and messages, letters, reports, reviews and instructions. In each case the task is fully contextualised and the purpose and intended recipient of the piece of writing is made clear.

It is the intention of the Writing paper to assess the student's ability to write in a register and style appropriate to the task and to present the work effectively. For this reason the tasks are fully fleshed out in order to encourage a well-focused response in a controlled context. It is essential for the student to comprehend fully the nature and detail of the task before attempting to tackle it. Students will lose marks if their answers do not fit the parameters laid down by the task.

In Section A there is no choice; all students must do the same task. There is usually a substantial reading input (up to 400 words) which students need to assimilate and they are asked to produce one or more pieces of writing in response to it. About 250 words are required in total.

The task asks the student to do one or more of the following: apply the given information, select and summarise, elicit information or compare parts of the input. As the task is so well-defined and all students must do this part of the paper, credit can be given for specific features and appropriate expression.

In Section B there is a choice between four tasks. Each task fully describes the required response. The purpose of the writing and the intended audience will be stated in each case. The tasks vary from articles and reports to letters, instructions and expanded notes. Students are asked to produce about 250 words, as for Section A.

Sometimes the tasks appear in an appropriate format, such as an advertisement or a form. However, the reading load is much lighter in this section of the paper – about 60 words per task in total. In any one test there will be a range of tasks and there is usually only one example of a particular type of writing.

If a particular form of response is required (e.g. a formal letter layout), this is indicated in the task.

Paper 3 English in Use

The English in Use paper is made up of three sections with about 75 questions in total. Each section will carry equal weighting.

In Section A there are two modified cloze passages. In the first passage the gaps in the text emphasise mainly lexical points and the student is asked to select a word from four options. In the second passage, the gaps are selected to test structural elements of the language. There are no options here and students must decide on the best word according to their understanding of the text. Each passage has 15 gaps and is about 200 words long.

The cloze passages aim to test the student's knowledge of the formal elements of the language in context. From a testing point of view these exercises are useful, if somewhat inauthentic, because they can assess a wide range of lexical and structural features of the language. Both texts come from original sources such as newspapers or periodicals but may be modified in some way to make them more accessible for students at this level.

In Section B there are usually two exercises. In the first exercise the students are asked to recognise and correct errors or inappropriate features from a range including spelling, lexis, style, textual organisation and punctuation. Some questions may focus on specific types of error such as word order or articles, etc. The second exercise usually asks the student to adapt a text or to alter the style or register in some way to make it more suitable for a particular purpose.

Both exercises are designed to test a student's ability to use the real-life skills of proof-reading or refining texts that could be required in study or at work. This section also encourages students to become aware of the need to correct and improve written work and enhance the skill of self-correction.

In Section C there are two exercises. One exercise usually asks the student to complete a gapped text with an appropriate phrase or sentence. This is designed to assess the student's understanding of cohesion within sentences and between paragraphs. The other exercise will usually ask the student to expand notes into a fuller form. Here the aim is to test the student's manipulation of given elements. The students should be encouraged to be careful and accurate rather than creative or imaginative in this sort of question.

Although many of the texts used in this paper come from original sources, the lexical level is carefully controlled and students are not expected to deal with topics in a way which demands a knowledge of the language above that already defined. Students are asked to transfer their answers onto OMR sheets as for Paper 1. Spaces allow for up to three-word answers. The last question is given appropriate space. One sample OMR sheet for Paper 3 (first page only) is provided at the back of the Student's Book.

Paper 4 Listening

The Listening paper is recorded on audio tape, as in FCE and CPE, and all the time needed to read the questions, write the answers and transfer these to the OMR sheets is included on the tape. This is why the tape lasts longer than the same component for FCE or CPE. The actual test time is about 30–32 minutes, as for CPE. The Listening paper carries equal weighting (20 per cent) with the other papers and there are between 40 and 50 questions, using multiple choice, gap fill or matching techniques.

A sample OMR sheet for Paper 4 is provided at the back of the Student's Book.

Sections A, C and D are heard twice and Section B *once only*. The delivery rate

Question aims and formats

is at a normal accessible speed and light accents (American, Australian, etc.) are used when appropriate. In most cases the spoken texts are re-recorded with actors as it is difficult to control the linguistic features in authentic recordings. There are, however, some 'vox pop' pieces which are clear and of sufficient density for testing purposes. Background noise is used at the beginning of a recording in order to contextualise the extract but is faded out before the text is tested.

Questions normally follow the order of information in the text and, as in the Reading paper, questions which test overall understanding will come towards the end of a set of questions.

The instructions on the question paper and the tape will be the same and their aim is to establish a context for the listening passage as well as to give students clear guidance for answering the questions. Most of the questions only require one- or two-word answers or a brief phrase. The length of the gap should indicate the length of the answer required.

Texts are based on the following types of listening material: radio broadcasts and announcements; conversations and discussions; speeches, talks and lectures; vox pop interviews.

In Section A there is a short text, usually a monologue, and students are asked questions which involve extracting specific information.

In Section B there is a short text which is heard once only. However, within the text there will be some repetition and students once again are required to extract information.

Section C is usually in the form of a dialogue or discussion and questions require an understanding of the gist or general impression, as well as the attitudes or points of view of the speakers.

Section D consists of a series of short extracts lasting about 10–30 seconds which are loosely linked by a theme. Questions test the student's ability to identify the speakers or source or the nature of the information they hear.

Paper 5 Speaking

The speaking component of the examination diverges more radically from FCE and CPE than the other components. The test aims to produce a sample of language from students which includes both interactional and transactional language. It is divided into four phases in order to draw out these different types of language.

The language of interaction is that which occurs in initiating and maintaining social relations. The language may be imprecise and the participants tend to speak in short turns as the aim is to develop the relationship and participants need to balance their input.

Transactional language, however, aims to pass on information to listeners who in turn must respond in order to show that the message is understood. It is important for the structuring of the language to be clear and often the turns at speaking are longer than in an interactional situation.

Of course real-life language does not fall neatly into these categories but the oral interview aims to test both types of language, and for this reason the CAE always examines the students in pairs. There are also two examiners – an interlocuter and an assessor – and this helps to make this normally subjective part of the examination more reliable.

Each part of the speaking test is designed to elicit either transactional or interactional language and it is the role of the interlocutor to guide the students through the tasks in order to produce an appropriate sample of their language.

The assessor, meanwhile, may concentrate on assessing the students according to the established criteria, although at the end of the test the assessor may participate in order to develop fully the interactive potential of the situation.

During any session the two examiners will exchange roles, but not during the examining of any one pair. The test will last 15 minutes.

The four phases of the speaking test are as follows:

Phase A   In this part mainly social language is tested while the students introduce or are introduced to each other and answer direct questions from the interlocutor about their interests and activities, etc.

Phase B   The interlocutor gives both students a visual prompt, such as a photograph or diagram. One of the students is asked to describe and comment on it in such a way as to help the other student see similarities and differences in their picture. The situation is then reversed and the other student is given a similar task. Transactional language is being tested here.

Phase C   In this part both students are given the same problem-solving task and are given about three minutes to reach agreement or to exchange different points of view. This phase is testing the skills of negotiation and collaboration which involve both transactional and interactional language.

          The tasks may fall into the categories of sequencing, ranking, comparing and contrasting.

Phase D   In this section the assessor joins the group and may take the opportunity to redress any imbalance in the amount of language elicited from the students. This part of the test develops the issues raised in Phase C and allows all the participants to extend the views and ideas expressed. It is expected that the two students talk in short turns as directed by the examiner.

          The aim of this phase is to allow the assessor and the interlocutor to 'fine-tune' their judgements and to refocus the interview if that has proved necessary.

Marking and grading

All five papers of the CAE examination carry equal weighting. Each of the five papers is marked out of a different total, but the scores will be scaled by computer so that each paper contributes 20 per cent to the total mark.

Each paper is marked in a slightly different way. Samples of OMR sheets for Papers 1, 3 and 4 appear at the back of the Student's Book.

The Reading paper is marked entirely by an optical mark reader (OMR). The OMR sheets are fed in and scanned by the reader which is programmed with the list of correct keys.

The Writing paper is marked by EFL examiners who are trained and monitored through a co-ordination process as for FCE and CPE. A table of descriptors is used to enable examiners to award a mark out of 5 for each section, giving a raw mark out of 10 for the paper as a whole (see p.15).

The English in Use paper is answered on an OMR sheet and the mainly brief answers are inserted in gaps which are large enough for two or three words or letters. The last question is given several lines. The OMR sheets are then marked by trained markers who will use a carefully constructed mark-scheme. They are supervised by EFL examiners who will monitor and moderate the marking process. The markers will fill in the lozenge-shaped spaces for the correct mark to be awarded for each question. Once again these are fed into and read by the optical mark reader.

The Listening paper is marked in a similar way to the English in Use paper and the more tightly controlled mark-scheme allows for a clerical marking process.

The Speaking paper is marked by two examiners, although only one mark is entered on the student's mark sheet. The mark is agreed between the two examiners. This OMR sheet is once again fed into the reader. See p.17 for more detail.

The score on the five components are added together by the computer after the correct weighting has been applied. The final 'aggregate' mark determines the student's grade.

The results slip

Each student receives a results slip which tells them what grade they have achieved. This is in the range from A through to E. A, B, and C are passing grades; D and E are failing grades.

Students who fail are given an indication of which papers were the weaker, while students who pass know which papers they do really well in. Very weak students receive an 'ungraded' result and this means they have performed very poorly in all components of the examination.

Assessment and marking of Paper 2   Writing

Paper 2   Writing – Sample answers

The following pieces of writing have been selected from students' answers produced during trialling. We have given marks based on the assessment criteria for the examination in order to help teachers in assessing the work of their own students. Brief explanatory notes have been added to show how we arrived at these marks.

Sample answer A

> c/o Colne College
> Grange Road
> Winterslow
> BK2 0PL
>
> 15th March 1990
>
> Mrs J Granger
> Hotel Dominion
> Race Road
> Weston
> Notts. NM6 7BW
>
> Dear Mrs. Granger,
>
> Thank you for your letter dated 15th January.
> I am very sorry I have to change the good program you have put up for us. I'm afraid our speaker can't come before Saturday, and the rest of the committe have decided to come Saturday morning. I will therefor like to book the rooms for Saturday 1st. September. We will now need 21 single rooms and 32 share twin rooms. All rooms with private facilities. One suite. I'm afraid I have to cancel and change your well chosed catering list aswell.
> The supper 31st August and breakfast and coffee 1st September will be canceled. If it is possible I would like the lunch to be served at 12 o'clock. There will be 8 vegetarians. It will be nice if we therefor can have our tea earlyer about 3.30 pm.
> I'm afraid the theatre trip wasn't very popular. I will have to cancel the trip, and would like to book a dining room for formal dinner in sted. If this is possible we will not use the Hotel's grill room.
> Breakfast 2nd September will be as your list.
> We have decided it's better to have smaller groups 4–6 for the seminar, if it's possible to have more seminar rooms of cause.
> I am really sorry to do all this changing please apologise this.
> I look forward to your reply.
>
> Yours sincerely

Marking and grading

> Colne College
> 17th March 1990
>
> Dear Robert,
>
> Thank you for your letter.
> I'm sorry this official visit came up. We wanted to keep you the whole weekend, but we are still very happy you are able to come Saturday. I have written a letter to Mrs. Granger at Hotel Dominion and rebooked the rooms for Friday and changed the meals as you suggested.
> I hope everything will be all right and looking forward to seeing you at Hotel Dominion.
>
> Best wishes

Question answered: Practice Test 1   Section A

Mark given: 3

Language lacks range and sophistication, and accuracy is variable. There is a concise and coherent attempt to achieve the task, but with at least one major error of fact. Style and register are appropriate to the note but not to the formal letter.

Sample answer B

> Winterslow Int. Club
>
> Date: 9.3.91
> Our Ref C/O/JJ
>
> Mrs Granger
> Hotel Dominion
> Race Rd, Weston
> Notts. NM6 7BW
>
> Dear Mrs Granger
>
> Thank you very much for your letter of 15th Jan., confirming the reservation for this year's conference. I am afraid there are some ammendments to the schedule as listed below:
>
> | | | |
> |---|---|---|
> | Accommodation: | Fri 31 Aug. | All rooms cancelled (inc. suite Dr Meads) |
> | | Sat 1 Sep. | 20 single rooms 32 shared twins |
> | Catering: | Fri 31 Aug. | please cancell |
> | | Sat 1 Sep. | No breakfast. Dr. Meads |
> | | | Lunch 63 guests (inc. 8 vegatarian) |
> | | | Dinner as lunch |

Marking and grading

Conference room A	6.00 to 7.30 pm
Seminar rooms	1.30 to 6.00 pm
Entertainment	all theatre booking cancelled

In addition, I would be very gratefull if you could arrange the lunch to be served at 12.00 noon, and tea at 3.30 pm.
Please accept my apologies for any inconvenience caused by these changes and should there be any query regarding the new arrangement please contact me.

Your sincerely

J.J. Conference organiser.

Dear Dr Meads

Thank you for note and I must say that we are all very sorry that you won't be able to attend, but as you suggested we could go through the whole schedule on Saturday, though it will be very intensive. I have written to the Dominion and rearranged the plan as you suggested. We look forward to seeing you on 1st Sept.
In the meantime all the best wishes for your plans.

J.J.

Question answered: Practice Test 1   Section A

Mark given: 5

Apart from 'slip of the pen' spelling errors, language is assured, natural and precise. (This candidate should do well at CPE!) The task is well-organised and the register is entirely appropriate. There are small errors or omissions of fact which might cause confusion in a real-life situation, but these are too slight to warrant the loss of a mark.

Sample answer C

Our company was created in collaboration by a public and a private bank in 1961. Since its creation, the company has changed its owner(s) twice. In 1983 with the government privatisation policy, the company was eventually bought by, HELKA OTOMOTIVE LTD, the current owner.
   When the company changed hand in 1983 it was employing only 600 workers. in 7 years this number went up to 6000 and the company has become the second biggest and successful factory in the otomotive sectory in the. Its budget is almost twice bigger than that of the government.
   At first, work was based on making only cars but now, the company has been making lorries and tunnel boring machines. Although its name seems British, our company is a multinational plant all around Europe even in Japan.
   As far as its routines are concerned, the work in the company is divided into two shifts; first one from 08.00 to 17.00 and second one from 17.30 to 02.30. Our workers have a meal and two 15 minute breaks during working hours. They also benefit from a 45 day holidays while they are still paid.

Marking and grading

> Our production process are based on three steps. In brief bodywork is made in the first step, in the second, workers fit engines and do accessory works then in the final step, cars are completed by painting and the necessary work. A completed car has to pass through quality control in order to be ready for sale.
> With new techonology, our capacity of production has remarkably increased, as a result now we are able to make 5000 cars, 275 heavy lorries and 25 tunnel boring machines per year.
> Our shares on the stockmarket are very valuable and reliant. Our 1989 profit is more than £10 billion. Our administration committe are about to work on new investments in other industries.
> Our personnel policy is based on the quality and ability of workers. The workers are singled out carefully, at the same time, they are paid very well.
> All Our ground which is situated on a 125,000 m² all around the world consists of some medical services, buffets, sports halls, restaurants even swimming pools.
> Our administration centre is in London. Neverthless the company has several branches and agents in Europe and in Japan.

Question answered: Practice Test 1   Section B   Question 1

Mark given: 4

Uses a good range of appropriate lexis, but other linguistic features are poorly controlled. The task is approached in a well-organised and authoritative manner, with a reasonable attempt at an appropriate register. The ending is rather weak.

Sample answer D

> Dear _____.
> Hello, I would like to advise you about my city and my house though you know that it is different from my country to yours about life style or culture and so on. So I suggest about them At first I advise how to live you can here. I have 5 bedrooms and 2 baths, toilet, kitchen, living room, and so on, you can use every room and you also are able to use ever funitures. so when you arrive here, you will are able to live easily. because. there are a lot of foreign people in my city and some of civilian are able to speak. English so Don't worry about your life there. In spite of you can't our language, you will be enjoy in your life. because We have a lot of place to play every sports and play ground in my city, but there are a lot of problems for you because you are stranger in my country so you will lost your way sometimes, but if you do so, you don't hesitate to ask to people your way or your adress. Almost of civilians are very kind for you. anyway I wrote every explanation, I put them in my house, so if you worry something, please read them. and so you also can call to me.
> Otherwise I don't have any advice in particular. but don't forget that you read my letter which is in my house and I wish you could be enjoy there for a month. and I'd like to have your advise about your hous and so on,
>
>   best wishes,
> your sincerilly

Question answered: Practice Test 1   Section B   Question 3

Mark given: 1

Marking and grading

Numerous language errors, many of which obscure meaning. Poor organisation and task not really tackled. (This candidate is not ready for CAE.)

Sample answer E

> The Management of the Grand Hotel welcomes you here in Gastein and hopes to make your stay most pleasant.
>
> With this little guide we try to give you a short information of the sparetime facilities we or public buildings offer throughout the year or just in summer or winter season.
>
> Gastein is specialized on families and so you can choose between a broad variety of offers. All the places are to reach either with public buses or the Grand Hotel Taxi Service are all to be found in the Gastein Valley.
>
> Culture: Every Monday from 4 to 6 pm there is a puppet-on-the-string theatre and as it also has famous plays in its' programme it is a pleasure for the whole family,
>
> Children's theatre, Bachweg 5 Gastein.
>
> Every day except Sunday from 10 a.m to 4 p.m you can visit a museum, which tells the story of many well-known cartoon characters and children have the possibility to make their own film every first Monday of the month.
>
> Museum of cartoons, Forellenweg 10, Badgastein.
>
> If you prefer to become activ in Sport instead you'll be glad about our offers below:
>
> Akorn sports centre: open from 10 a.m to 6. pm. offers many kinds of in- and outdoor Sports.
>
> Very popular are table-tennis, tennis, soccer, volleyball and swimming. It's also possible to give your child into the care of a spezial trained person and 'explore' the centre on your own.
>
> In Gastein you can also go for long walks through unspoilt Austrian countryside or just take the cable-car up to one of the mountains and enjoy the view over the land-scape.
>
> In winter Gastein is very popular for skiing and skating and special courses to reasonable prizes are offered for children and adult beginners. The local icerink starts in November and is open daily from 1 to 6 p.m. For nearer information how to get there see the map below.
>
> In the Hillside park is a big playing ground and every Sunday at 10 a.m. starts a workshop for children with interesting topics.
>
> The Management hopes to have given you a short information, if we can help you in any way please don't hesitate to ask us we'll be pleased to fullfill your wishes
>
> The Management

Question answered: Practice Test 2   Section B   Question 1

Mark given: 3

Attempts a good range of structure and lexis, but L1 interference causes awkwardness at several points. With regard to the task, it is a complete and well-organised answer, appropriate in tone and register.

Marking and grading

Sample answer F

> 5B Margaret's Road
> OXFORD.
> OX2 6SP
>
> 26th November 1990
>
> Dear Nadia,
>   How are you? I'm fine.
>   I'm writing you about the camera that you've borroweed to me for my English holidays. I'm really sorry but I have to tell you an awufful news, your camera is damaged.
>   I don't know how that could be happened. Last Saturday I decided to go to London with some friends and I put your camera in my bag. We took the ten o'clock train to London and we walked around the city all the day. In London there were so many people that sometimes I've got problems to keep my bag safety. During the day I've taken many photographes and the camera was in order. We came back to Oxford in the latest afternoon and the seats in the train were all busy, we've had to stay up and I've laid my bag on the floor. When I arrived in my room I emptied my bag and I found that your camera was serious damaged.
>   Now I've decided to buy another camera, like yours, and when I'll come back to Switzerland I'll give you that one instade of the other.
>   Please let me know if you agree with this solution.
>   Best wishes,

Question answered: Practice Test 3   Section B   Question 4

Mark given: 2

Language marred by relatively basic inaccuracies. Task not well-developed (rather short).

Paper 2 Writing – Assessment criteria

This table shows the typical features of work gaining each mark. These include quality of language (i.e. grammar, lexis, spelling, punctuation, syntax) and task achievement (i.e. content, organisation, relevance, completeness, cohesion, style, register).

5	Totally positive effect on target reader. Minimal errors. Resourceful, controlled and natural use of language showing a good range of vocabulary and structure. Completion of task: well-organised, good use of cohesive devices, appropriate register, no relevant omissions.
4	Sufficiently natural, errors only when more complex language attempted. Some evidence of range of vocabulary and structure. A good attempt at achieving the task. Any omissions are only minor. Attention paid to organisation and cohesion; register not always natural but positive effect on target reader achieved.
3	Use of English satisfactory, though lacking range and variety. Occasional serious errors should not impede communication although patience required of reader. Task reasonably attempted with some organisation and cohesion. No significant irrelevancies.
2	Errors sometimes obscure communication and/or language too elementary. Some attempt at task but notable omissions and/or lack of organisation and cohesion would have negative effect on reader.
1	Serious lack of control and/or frequent basic errors. Narrow range of language. Totally inadequate attempt at task.
0	Not sufficient comprehensible language for assessment.

Assessment and marking of Paper 5   Speaking

Criteria

There are five criteria for assessment. The brief descriptors on the grid should be read in conjunction with the notes given below.

Fluency

This relates to the naturalness of the speed and rhythm, together with the lack of hesitations and pauses. Pauses to marshal thoughts rather than language should be regarded as natural features of spoken interaction and not penalised.

Accuracy

This refers to the range (quantity) and correctness (quality) of both grammatical structures and vocabulary. Major errors (i.e. those which obscure the message) should be penalised more heavily than minor ones (i.e. those which do not obscure the message). Obvious or self-corrected slips of the tongue should not be penalised.

Pronunciation

This covers both individual sounds and prosodic or utterance-level features such as stress-timing, rhythm, placing of stress, intonation patterns, and range of pitch within utterances. It is not expected that candidates' pronunciation should be entirely free of L1 features, even at band 8.

Task achievement

This scale refers to candidates' participation in the four phases of the Speaking paper and covers the following areas:
– fullness of candidate's contributions
– appropriacy or relevance of contributions to the tasks
– independence in carrying out the tasks set (i.e. the degree to which candidates can carry out the tasks without prompting or redirection by the interlocutor or the other candidate)
– the organisation of the candidate's contributions (logical or coherent sequencing of utterances)
– a candidate's flexibility or resourcefulness
– the degree to which a candidate's language contributes to successful task management through the selection of appropriate language functions and vocabulary.

The attempt to complete the tasks is what is being assessed; failure to reach a 'right' or complete answer within the time available should not be penalised.

Interactive communication

This refers to a candidate's ability to interact both actively and responsively, and includes the candidate's sensitivity to the norms of turn-taking appropriate to each phase of the paper. Aggression, deliberate dominance or intimidation should be penalised; a candidate whose partner behaves in such a way should not be penalised. Candidates who are unwilling or unable to take their turns adequately will receive a reduced score on this scale.

The mark bands

Teachers may find it helpful to compare the CAE Paper 5 mark bands with the standards expected at CPE and FCE.

7–8 band   Candidates scoring 7 or 8 would probably also be capable of passing CPE.
5–6 band   Very good FCE candidates might achieve such marks, at their very best.
3–4 band   A narrow fail at CAE, but probably a pass at FCE.
1–2 band   A clear fail at CAE and probably at FCE too.

Paper 5   Speaking – Assessment criteria

This table shows the typical oral features gaining these marks.

	Fluency	Accuracy	Pronunciation	Task achievement	Interactive communication
7–8	Coherent spoken interaction with good speed and rhythm. Few intrusive hesitations.	Evidence of a wide range of structures and vocabulary. Errors minimal in number and gravity.	Little L1 accent / L1 accent not obtrusive. Good mastery of English pronunciation features.	The tasks are dealt with fully and effectively. The language is appropriate to each task.	Contributes fully and effectively throughout the interaction.
5–6	Occasional but noticeable hesitations, but not such as to strain the listener or impede communication.	Evidence of a good range of structures and vocabulary. Errors few in number and minor in gravity. These errors do not impede communication.	Noticeable L1 accent having minor difficulties with some pronunciation features. These do not strain the listener or impede communication.	The tasks are mostly dealt with effectively but with minor inadequacies of execution or language.	Contributes with ease for most of the interaction, with only occasional and minor difficulties.
3–4	Fairly frequent and noticeable hesitations. Communication is achieved but strains the listener at times.	Fairly frequent errors and evidence of restricted range of structures and/or vocabulary. These do not prevent communication of the essential message.	Obvious L1 pronunciation features with major defects. These may strain the listener and/or make comprehension of detail difficult.	One or more of the tasks are dealt with in a limited manner. The language is often inappropriate. Redirection may have been required at times.	Contributes effectively for some of the interaction, but fairly frequent difficulties.
1–2	Disconnected speech and/or frequent hesitations impede communication and strain the listener.	Frequent basic errors and limited range of structures and/or vocabulary impede communication and strain the listener.	Heavy L1 pronunciation and widespread difficulties with English features impede communication of the message and strain the listener.	Inadequate attempts at the tasks using little appropriate language. Requires major redirection or assistance.	Difficulty in maintaining contributions throughout. May respond to simple or structured interaction but obvious limitations in freer situations.
0	Sample of language inadequate for assessment (even after prompting by the interlocutor).				

Preparing students for CAE

Paper 1 Reading

Many students will initially find the high reading load for this paper very daunting. It is important therefore that careful, step-by-step preparation is employed to bring them to the stage where they can confidently tackle a whole paper in one hour.

Before focusing on reading at speed, ensure that students are equipped to extract information from all aspects of a text. If practicable, familiarise them with a variety of printed materials: guidebooks, textbooks, periodicals, brochures, newspapers, etc. If this is difficult, use EFL sources which present authentic reading texts in their original layout. Teach your students to observe headlines, typeface, page layout, punctuation, etc. as a guide to provenance and register *before* reading, and to observe lexical and structural clues *while* they read.

Draw students' attention to the variety of question types used and encourage them to use the question format as a guide to the *type* of reading skill being tested. For example, questions preceding the text indicate that the text should be scanned for specific information. It is a waste of time to plod through every last word (e.g. Practice Test 2, Paper 1, First text).

Multiple-matching exercises (e.g. Practice Test 1, Paper 1, First text; Practice Test 4, Paper 1, Second text) on the other hand, require close reading of the text. It will often be useful for students to underline the relevant parts of the text (e.g. Practice Test 1, Paper 1, First text, the *names* listed A–E), during the first read through, to save time searching while they complete the matching exercise. Multiple-matching exercises lend themselves particularly well to pair or group work, as a basis for discussion, and it is advisable to give students several practice sessions in a relaxed classroom context so that they are not disconcerted by having to do such an exercise alone for the first time.

Paragraph gapping (e.g. Practice Test 1, Paper 1, Fourth text) is a test of students' understanding of the text as a whole, its structure and coherence. Advise students to read the gapped text, skipping the gaps, to form a general idea of how it develops. Train them to observe internal signs (such as use of pronouns, sequencing adverbials) to check how the given paragraphs fit, in addition to judging by their content. This type of exercise can be prepared for by students in small groups: they write straightforward narratives of five short paragraphs. They copy paragraphs 1, 3 and 5 on to another paper and hand it to a classmate. The other student must fill the gaps with invented paragraphs. These can be compared with the originals. Alternatively, the narrative may be cut into paragraphs and a traditional sequencing exercise carried out.

Paper 2 Writing

The writing tasks which students are set in this paper are always contextualised. The students therefore know not only *what* they must write (e.g. a letter, a report), but also for *whom* they are writing, and *why*. This releases both students and teachers from having to practise 'essays' which serve no purpose other than demonstrating command of formal writing conventions. However, contextualisation of tasks means that students must be able to gauge the style and register appropriate to a range of situations and produce suitable written work. Learning to judge how to write, as well as what to write, can usefully be linked to work for the Reading paper, although the level of language which students are expected to produce is not, of course, the same as that which they should be able to understand.

Section A

This compulsory exercise is designed to allow students maximum scope to demonstrate their ability to express themselves in writing, by providing all the necessary information. Two ground rules must be observed in practising this type of task. First, the information must not be altered, although it may be added to; second, some information will probably have to be ignored, as irrelevant to the given task. Students should be advised first of all to spend adequate time on analysing the task so that they are absolutely clear about what they have to do. They should then mark up the text, picking out essential information and making connections where relevant. It will usually be a good idea to sketch a brief sequential plan as well, incorporating any additional ideas of their own. This will enable them to concentrate on the accuracy and appropriacy of their language as they write. It will be very useful, and productive, to take students through the three preparatory stages, outlined above, in class, before they settle to write on their own. The preparation can be done first of all as a teacher-led activity, then by students working in groups or in pairs, as they become more confident.

Section B

In this section, students must draw largely on their own imagination, experience, or knowledge. As in Section A, it is important that careful analysis of the task is undertaken in order to pinpoint the purpose and context of the writing. Otherwise students may produce work which, although interesting and accurate, is marked down because it is inappropriate. This is especially true of some tasks which *appear* very simple. For example, in Practice Test 1, Paper 2, Section B, Question 3, students may feel secure because they are certain that they know the locality in which they live. However, the information they give must be factual, detailed and organised. The letter may be 'informal', but this does not imply that a casual description, with a few airy phrases about 'you can hire a car' amid enthusiastic descriptions of scenery, will answer the question. This sort of task is deceptive. Sometimes an apparently more challenging one will in fact turn out to be quite straightforward.

It should be noted that Section B does not normally contain a question which requires the same form and register as Section A. That is, if Section A requires an

Preparing students for CAE

informal letter, there will not be one in Section B; if Section A requires a report, there will not be one in Section B, and so on. Students must be prepared to write both formal and informal language.

Paper 3   English in Use

Section A

The two modified cloze exercises in this section can be approached in different ways. It will help students to spend class time developing an appropriate pattern for each. These could be:

1. *Lexical cloze*
   Step 1: Read through text quickly to get overall picture.
   Step 2: Answer item by item, using contextual clues where appropriate.

2. *Structural cloze*
   Step 1: Read through (as above).
   Step 2: *Attempt* to fill gaps, checking context *before and after* for clues.
   Point out that: (a) gaps are sometimes interdependent, e.g. . . . *so small that . . .*;
   (b) if stuck, ignore gap and go on – it may be easier when the text is more or less complete.

N.B. For both cloze exercises, students should remember *never* to leave blanks, however uncertain they are. Guesses *can* be right, blanks cannot!

Section B

The skills tested in both parts of Section B can be practised in teaching exercises which may form part of the class routine.

3. *Error correction*
   Students should be encouraged to check their own, or colleagues', work. Checking for specific types of error can be integrated with study of particular aspects of language, for example, punctuation (Practice Test 2, Paper 3, Question 3) or spelling (Practice Test 3, Paper 3, Question 3).

4. *Amending style or register*
   Students may be asked to write informal notes on a given subject and then to exchange texts and amend each other's notes. This kind of exercise can form a useful introduction to considerations of the language used in different contexts, which is also relevant to the Writing paper.

Section C

These exercises may be used in lessons where students are studying the structure of language, especially at clause level.

5. *Text completion*
   Students should be encouraged to observe and employ the variety of devices which link and order a text. It is usually best to begin practice at a basic level, joining simple clauses to form complex sentences, using relative pronouns

and so on. This kind of exercise can be used to practise structural accuracy, for example when studying the formation and sequencing of tenses, word order (e.g. adjectives and adverbials), or the use of articles and other determiners. Again, it is probably best to begin with sentences and work up to longer texts.

Paper 4 Listening

For this paper, students need both dedicated practice to learn specific listening strategies and exposure to as much and as varied spoken language as possible. For students not in an English-speaking environment, this exposure may be very difficult to achieve. Students should be given every encouragement to listen to English outside the classroom (see suggestions in Student's Book, pages 2–3).

As far as technique is concerned, familiarity with the formats in these practice tests and careful attention to rubrics will enable students to concentrate on the meanings and implications relevant to individual tasks. Encourage students to use the time before they hear the texts wisely. They should try to predict the topic and use the questions as prompts while listening. They should also be reassured that minor errors of written language (e.g. spelling) will be ignored, provided the meaning of their answer is clear.

Section A is normally a straightforward, informational text, heard twice. The questions often offer helpful clues about the text, and students should be aware of this.

Section B may need more practice as it is heard only once. Students should learn to listen for the repetitions *within* the text.

Section C may be linked to oral practice. The speaker(s) will generally be expressing feelings and attitudes rather than giving information. Stress and intonation exercises may be based on sections of text, or used as a lead-in to the listening work.

Section D can often be presented as a class exercise. For example, before hearing the rubric, the class can be asked to guess the theme. Afterwards students can be asked to choose one speaker and develop the utterance further in mini role-playing exercises.

Paper 5 Speaking

Because speaking skills are tested with pairs of candidates, it is relatively easy to incorporate examination practice into class activities. Specific exam preparation need cover little more than an explanation of the four phases (see page 7, and materials for the Speaking paper within each test). The social, interactional and transactional language required can be practised in the pair-work phase of oral lessons, using the visual prompts provided. This can also form the basis of valuable writing exercises, as follow-up work. For example, after using the pictures of animals in Practice Test 1 for oral pair work, there could be a class discussion on keeping animals in captivity, with written homework in the form of a report or letter to a newspaper.

Practice Test 1

Paper 1 Reading   (1 hour)

First text: 1. E   2. D   3. A   4. C   5. B   6. E   7. D
8. A   9. A   10. F   11. D   12. E   13. B   14. C

Second text: 15. B   16. A   17. G   18. F   19. E   20. D

Third text: 21. B   22. A   23. B   24. B   25. D

Fourth text: 26. A   27. D   28. A   29. B   30. B   31. C
32. A   33. D   34. C   35. B   36. A   37. A

Paper 2 Writing   (2 hours)

See pages 9–15 for assessment criteria and sample answers.

Paper 3 English in Use   (1 hour 30 minutes)

Section A

Question 1   [One mark for each correct answer]

1. C   2. A   3. D   4. B   5. D   6. A   7. C   8. A
9. C   10. A   11. D   12. C   13. D   14. A   15. A

Question 2   [One mark for each correct answer]

1. for   2. himself/herself/themselves   3. if/when(ever)/where(ever)
4. to   5. makes   6. best/only   7. just/only/pitched/and/raised
8. than   9. rather/more   10. without   11. even/may/also/might/often/can   12. better/only   13. but   14. more   15. by

Section B

Question 3   [One mark for each correct answer]

1. As   2. other   3. more   4. who   5. of   6. the
7. about   8. up   9. always   10. to   11. even   12. the
13. in

Practice Test 1

Question 4 [One mark for each correct answer]

1. talking about   2. the dangers   3. will be   4. his collection
5. willing / there / on hand / here   6. to make / in   7. pieces of
8. set in / about/on   9. the meeting   10. on / Tuesday / on Tuesday the
11. (are) available / can be bought   12. on Hexton   13. on / at the

Section C

Question 5 [One mark for each correct answer]

1. J   2. N   3. G   4. O   5. F   6. I   7. K   8. L
9. P   10. M   11. B

Question 6

Here is a sample answer:

> Dear Susan,
>
> I've now managed to find the time to visit the school where you think you might send Timothy next year, so I'll try and give you as much information as possible.
>
> a) The school itself is modern. I should think it was built about five years ago and there are several buildings set in large grounds and surrounded by trees. [2 marks]
>
> b) The headmistress met me and showed me round the classrooms and laboratories. [2 marks]
>
> c) There are at least twelve large classrooms (which seemed very light and airy) as the windows overlook the grounds. [2 marks]
>
> d) There is a biology laboratory and a physical science laboratory which seem to be well equipped with all the latest gadgets. [2 marks]
>
> e) There is a swimming pool which is heated and as it's inside they can give swimming lessons all the year round. [2 marks]
>
> f) I was impressed by the staff who seemed interested and friendly and obviously have good relations with the children. [2 marks]
>
> g) The pupils, too, were a happy lot and I was surprised how quiet everything was! I think the discipline must be quite good. [2 marks]
>
> h) I didn't have time to see where the children live. The headmistress assured me that children who were a long way from home quickly settled down and [2 marks]
>
> i) the staff took great care to make sure that they felt happy and secure. Anyway, I think I would recommend it and suggest you pay the school a visit as soon as possible. [2 marks]
>
> Best wishes,

[Total: 18 marks]

Practice Test 1

Paper 4 Listening (45 minutes)

Section A   [One mark for each correct answer]

1. ✓   2. £8.50   3. ✓   4. ✓   5. ✓   6. £10   7. –   8. ✓
9. ✓   10. £6–7   11. ✓   12. ✓

[Total: 12 marks]

Section B   [One mark for each correct answer]

13. Exlux   14. VC450D   15. electrical   16. dust bag
17. nearest/nearby/local   18. replace (*not* repair)   19. plug
20. disposable/paper bag(s) [½+½ marks]   21. (a) fire

[Total: 9 marks]

Section C   [One mark for each correct answer]

22. the real person
23. she thought of him as a project
24. a) was very young / was too young / was only 20
    b) go dancing / dance
25. hard, tough, unjust, etc.
26. visit her / keep in touch / find out how she was / worry about her
27. little and cuddly / small and cuddly
28. close / close to one another (*do not accept* closed)
29. hers / hers alone / up to her / up to her alone / just hers / in her hands

[Total: 9 marks]

Section D   [One mark for each correct answer]

Task 1:   30. C   31. D   32. B   33. A   34. F
Task 2:   35. B   36. G   37. F   38. E   39. C

[Total: 10 marks]

Transcript

You have been given a question paper for the Certificate in Advanced English, Test One. There are four parts to this test, Sections A, B, C and D. You will hear each part twice, except for Section B which will be heard once only. There will be pauses to allow you to look through the questions before each part, and other pauses to let you think about your answers. At the end of every pause you will hear this sound.

tone

The tape will now be stopped while you look at your question paper. You must ask any questions now, as you will not be allowed to speak during the test.

[*pause*]

Section A. You will hear a woman calling the Tourist Information Office in a town called Halifax where she is organising a meeting. She wants to book lunch and dinner at different restaurants and she wants to find out what they can offer. For questions 1–12 tick the boxes or put in the prices while you are listening to the conversation. Some of the boxes have been filled in for you and you will find it necessary to leave some boxes blank. Listen carefully. You will hear the piece twice.

[*pause*]

tone

Tourist office receptionist:	Hello, this is the tourist office. Can I help you?
Client:	Yes, please. I want to find out some details about restaurants in Halifax. I need to arrange lunch and dinner for a group of overseas representatives who are visiting our factory. I have heard that The Bull's Head offers set lunches?
Receptionist:	Yes, now, let me see. The Bull's Head can offer you a set lunch, excluding wine for £8.50 per head, including a vegetarian option.
Client:	Is that in the main restaurant?
Receptionist:	Yes, it is, but they do offer a private room for large groups over 20. Now, £8.50 seems good value to me.
Client:	There will be at least 24 of them, so I expect the private room would be better.
Receptionist:	Now Bruiseyard's restaurant in Hooper Street can also offer a set lunch with wine for £10 but there isn't anything particularly suitable for vegetarians. But it is good value at £10, I'd say. This would be in the main restaurant, but you would need to book early. I see they also offer dinner for large groups but this is much more expensive – £15 per head, not including wine but a five course menu including plenty of variety for those who don't eat meat.
Client:	Is there anything cheaper? It's going to be pretty expensive if you add wine to that £15 per dinner.
Receptionist:	Well, there's the Arts Theatre restaurant – it's above the theatre in the Market Square. It offers lunches and dinners and it's very reasonable and can cater for large numbers if you give them warning. I believe you could get lunch for about £6 or £7 per person and dinner for about £10 and there would be no problem for vegetarians.
Client:	£6 to £7 sounds good to me. Is there a separate room from the main restaurant?
Receptionist:	No, but they can offer what they call 'party service' which means you'll be given a large table and waited on separately. There's a small cover charge for that. You'd need to tell them in advance if you wanted the vegetarian menu.
Client:	Well, thank you. I've got a lot to think about.
Receptionist:	Good, that's fine. Do ring again if you have any further queries.

[*pause*]

Practice Test 1

tone

Now you will hear the piece again. [The recording is repeated.]

[*pause*]

That is the end of Section A.

[*pause*]

Section B. You will hear a report on the radio warning people to check if they have a certain kind of vacuum cleaner which has proved faulty. As you have recently bought one, you note down the details. Complete the notes by writing one or two words in the spaces numbered 13–21. Listen carefully as you will hear this piece once only.

[*pause*]

tone

Now here is a report about a possible fault with an Exlux vacuum cleaner. If you have recently bought an Exlux vacuum cleaner from any branch of Hixons – Model No. VC 450D, please check the following, as there may be an electrical fault which could be dangerous. If the model features a reusable dust bag (some models require disposable bags), there may well be a fault in the manufacture. You are asked to return the cleaner to your nearest branch of Hixons or call them on 081 447 260 and they will collect and replace it for you. Whatever you do, don't plug it in and attempt to use it and don't try and fit paper bags – that is, disposable bags. They aren't suitable and could cause a fire.

[*pause*]

tone

That is the end of Section B.

[*pause*]

Section C. You are going to hear an interview with a woman called Gemma talking about her family. Complete the sentences 22–29 with a few words, using the information you hear. Now read the sentences and then listen carefully. You will hear the interview twice.

[*pause*]

tone

Interviewer:	More than anyone I've interviewed, Gemma, you have already discussed, in public, almost everything about yourself. I wonder whether you feel there is in any sense a private part of yourself?
Gemma:	There probably isn't. I don't think there's a little, frightened, weeping girl inside me somewhere that somebody ought to rescue and be kind to.
Interviewer:	Is that what is meant by private?
Gemma:	I don't know. I've never understood what people mean when they talk about going deeper into other people. It's as though people were like onions and you could go through layer after layer and finally get to a tiny layer and inside that is the real person. It seems to me that what you learn about people is not by getting deeper into them or closer to them; people reveal all sorts of bits of themselves in different ways and in different encounters.
Interviewer:	How long had you planned to write a book about your father?

Gemma: Ever since I can remember. I think that was part of his problem with me: I always looked at him as I would a project I had to get to work on.

Interviewer: Are you saying that you suspected there was a secret about him?

Gemma: Well, I'd say to him, 'Why don't I have grandparents on your side of the family, where are they?', and sometimes he'd say that they were in England and sometimes he'd say they were dead.

Interviewer: And when as a child you asked your mother, what did she reply to those questions about your father?

Gemma: I don't think I ever asked her.

Interviewer: Why not?

Gemma: Well, I had a very bad relationship with my mother. She was very young when I was born – barely 20.

Interviewer: Was her relationship with your sister Jane and your brother Barry better?

Gemma: Oh, totally. I was a disaster for her. She hadn't wanted a baby that early, although I was born more than two years after she married. What she wanted was to dance on the deck of an ocean liner, under the stars, to the strain of Nelson Riddle.

Interviewer: You're fairly tough on her.

Gemma: There's something funny about my mother's ego structure. She literally doesn't care what people think about her. She seems to have no super ego; you can't appeal to her finer feelings. She alternates in her moods between extreme vulnerability, and seeing herself as very inadequate and unable to cope, and extraordinary arrogance, regarding everyone else as a fool.

Interviewer: What does your mother make of you? At times, in what you've written, you make it sound as if she doesn't make anything of you really – you just engaged in activities that mystify her. Is that because you threaten her?

Gemma: I'm sure I do, but I would threaten her for lots of reasons. Guilt is just one of them.

Interviewer: Now, about the relationship with your father. Someone said to me, very critically, 'Oh, well, she never saw her father from the time she left Australia to the time he was dying.' Had you gone back to Australia? Did you see him?

Gemma: My relationship with Australia parallels my relationship with my father. I first left home when I was 17, but had to return because I was too young to stay away and I hadn't enough money to live on or anywhere to live. When I was 18 I left for good. My father never made the slightest attempt to see where I was or whether I was well or sick. Then when I got my scholarship to Cambridge I went home to say goodbye to my family.

Interviewer: Did your father love you?

Gemma: I don't know, I think he probably loved me when I was a baby, but children often get a lot of love when they're little and cuddly, but when they get older it's suddenly different, especially when there's a little brother or sister. People say, 'Oh well, you weren't very close to your father', but in our society now it's practically impossible to be close to your father.

Interviewer: Let me ask you one last thing. Having written the book about your father, have you found that it's changed you?

Gemma: I think it's changed me fundamentally. I really didn't understand until it happened how devastating the death of a parent is; even a parent who

Practice Test 1

is rather distant. Your spiritual horizon changes completely. It's suddenly you holding back the tide. You're the guardian of the coming generations and all the responsibility is yours. You no longer have to account to anyone. You're it.

[*pause*]

tone

Now you will hear the piece again. [The recording is repeated.]

[*pause*]

That is the end of Section C.

[*pause*]

Section D. In a few moments you will hear various people talking. There are five extracts which are not related in any way except that everyone is talking about the environment. Task One lists the people who speak on the tape and Task Two lists what they are talking about. It is better to concentrate on Task One during the first hearing and Task Two during the second hearing. For Task One look at the people labelled A–H. As you listen, decide in what order you hear each person speak and complete the boxes 30–34 with the appropriate letter. For Task Two look at the topics labelled A–H and put them in the order in which you hear them by completing the boxes 35–39 with the appropriate letter. Listen carefully. You will hear the people twice.

[*pause*]

tone

Member of the Green Party:
Individually, we have to take responsibility for what we do. That means shutting doors and not heating the whole house. It means dressing sensibly and using public transport.

Farmer:
A lot of people grumble and say we are ruining the countryside but without modern methods there would be no cheap food. We need big fields without obstacles like trees and hedges so we can use large, fast machinery. That way you get a better harvest.

Interview in supermarket:
Woman: Well, I wouldn't buy that environmentally friendly stuff – it's too expensive. Anyway I'm sure it doesn't wash as well. It's only soap, isn't it?
Interviewer: But it won't hurt the environment, will it? That's good, isn't it?
Woman: Well, that's what the manufacturers say. I want more proof . . .

Representative from chemical company:
But we've been thinking about the state of the environment for years. Each substance that we produce is tested carefully before going on sale. We know they are safe if they are used properly.

Phone call to council officer responsible for waste-disposal:
Man: It's your dustbin men again. They've dropped disgusting bits from my dustbin all down the passage. I want to know what you're going to do about it.

Practice Test 1

Council Official: I'm sorry sir, but if you'll let me have your address I shall send someone round to clear up the mess as soon as possible.
Man: That's all very well, but . . .

[*pause*]

tone

Now you will hear the piece again. [The recording is repeated.]

[*pause*]

That is the end of Section D. There will now be a pause to allow you to check your work.

[*pause*]

That is the end of the test.

Paper 5 Speaking   (15 minutes)

Note: In the examination, there will be both an assessor and an interlocutor in the room. The following notes use plural forms where appropriate, although we realise that a teacher may often be working alone for practice sessions.

You will need to refer to Paper 5 of Practice Test 1 in the Student's Book and the colour section 'Visual materials for Paper 5, Phase B' also in the Student's Book.

Phase A   (approximately three minutes)

Interlocutor or assessor:
   Good morning. My name is . . . and this is my colleague . . .
   And your names are?
   First of all we'd like to know a little about you. Do you know each other?

If yes:
   So perhaps you (Candidate A) could tell us about (Candidate B). Where's s/he from? What does s/he do? What are his/her hobbies?
   And (Candidate B), would you like to tell us about (Candidate A) now, please?
   How long have you known each other?
   What do you know about each other's country?

If no:
   Could you please find out about each other? Talk about where you're from, what you do, what you're interested in, and so on.
   Is there any special reason why you're studying English?
   What plans do you have for your future?

The questions in Phase A may be varied considerably according to the context, but will always cover introductions and general social conversation, following approximately the structure set out above.

Practice Test 1

Phase B (three or four minutes)

1 | SOCIAL GATHERINGS (Compare and contrast) |

Int: *In this part of the test I'm going to give each of you a picture to look at. Please do not show your pictures to each other. (Candidate A) I'd like you to look at picture 1A.*

Show picture **1A** to Candidate A.

Now, (Candidate B), will you look at picture 1B?

[To Candidate A] *I'd like you to describe your picture to (Candidate B) who has a picture which is similar to yours but not the same. Describe it fully and after about a minute I'll ask (Candidate B) to say how far his/her picture is different from and the same as yours.*
[To Candidate B] *Here's some spare paper in case you want to make any notes. All right?*
So (Candidate A), would you start please?

APPROXIMATELY ONE MINUTE

Thank you. Now, (Candidate B), I'd like you to tell (Candidate A) briefly how your picture is different from and the same as his/hers.

APPROXIMATELY 20 SECONDS

Now, would you like to compare the pictures?

ALLOW A FEW SECONDS, THEN PASS TO PHASE B2

2 | ANIMALS (Select one from many) |

In this part of the test I'm going to give you some pictures to look at. Please look at page C3.

Make sure that both candidates are looking at ANIMALS, pictures **1C–1H**.

Indicate one picture to Candidate B, ensuring that Candidate A does not know which one it is.

[To Candidate B] *I'd like you to describe this picture to (Candidate A). You have about a minute to do this.*

[To Candidate A] *I'd like you to listen and decide which picture is being described. If you are still uncertain when (Candidate B) has finished, you may ask him/her some questions to help you identify the picture. Otherwise, say briefly what helped you decide.*

APPROXIMATELY ONE MINUTE FOR THE DESCRIPTION

Phase C (approximately four minutes)

> CARING FOR THE ENVIRONMENT

Indicate the list of suggestions (pp. 28–9 in Student's Book) to both candidates.

Here are some suggestions for helping to take care of the environment. Discuss with your partner whether you think these are useful things to do and why. Then decide what order of importance you would put them in so that they would have most effect on the environment. You must reach agreement or 'agree to differ'. After four minutes you must report your decision.

APPROXIMATELY FOUR MINUTES FOR DISCUSSION

Phase D (approximately four minutes)

What did you decide was most important?
Why?
How far did you agree?
What did you disagree about? Why?
How could you encourage people to act in the ways mentioned?
In what ways would you like to see the environment being cared for in your country?
etc.

Practice Test 2

Paper 1 Reading   (1 hour)

First text: 1. J   2. A   3. C   4. A   5. D   6. F   7. A
8. E   9. F   10. H   11. D   12. H   13. B   14. D   15. H

Second text: 16. B   17. C   18. E   19. A   20. C   21. D
22. E   23. B

Third text: 24. A   25. F   26. C   27. B   28. B   29. F
30. C   31. A

Fourth text: 32. A   33. B   34. C   35. B   36. D   37. C

Paper 2 Writing   (2 hours)

See pages 9–15 for assessment criteria and sample answers.

Paper 3 English in Use   (1 hour 30 minutes)

Section A

Question 1   [One mark for each correct answer]

1. C   2. B   3. D   4. D   5. A   6. B   7. C   8. C
9. D   10. A   11. D   12. B   13. C   14. C   15. A

Question 2   [One mark for each correct answer]

1. were   2. many   3. for/very/too   4. on   5. them   6. to
7. began/started   8. first   9. one   10. only   11. until
12. by/to   13. that   14. under   15. with

Section B

Question 3   [One mark for each correct answer]

Thirty years ago men and women in Japan could expect to live for 64 and 68 years respectively – substantially less than the corresponding life expectations in England and Wales of 68 and 73. As we enter the 1990s the Japanese have achieved great improvements in their health. Life expectancy there is now 75 and 81 years. Here in

Britain the figures are 72 and 78. How have they managed to overtake us in health terms? An answer to this question was attempted in an article in the *British Medical Journal* (23–30 December 1989, p. 1547) by Professor Michael Marmot and Dr George Davey Smith. They were able to reject some possibilities. The Japanese don't spend a lot more money on health care than the British. They are not genetically healthier (Japanese who live in the United States are as prone to heart attacks as the Americans). The most important differences between Japan and Britain, the article concludes, are the diet and social class contrasts.

Question 4 [One mark for each correct answer]

1. to/from   2. surrounded by / with   3. too/as well
4. lots of/plenty of/loads of, etc.   5. including / as well as   6. as they
7. provided/there/available   8. ask for   9. nearly every
10. (on) some   11. integral / their own / your own   12. There is / There's

Section C

Question 5 [One mark for each correct answer]

1. B   2. E   3. A   4. I   5. M   6. G   7. P   8. F
9. K   10. L

Question 6

Here is a sample answer:

	Dear Sir,
a)	I recently took a holiday with Kephalonia Travel Ltd. for two weeks in July, flying from Gatwick Airport.
b)	However, the plane was delayed for four hours and yet we were given no information and the staff at the airport were most unhelpful. [2 marks]
c)	When we finally got on the plane the flight was terribly uncomfortable. There was only cold food served by a very rude air-hostess. [2 marks]
d)	We landed at midnight but there was no bus to meet us and so we had to hire a taxi which was quite expensive. When we did reach the hotel it was closed for the night. [2 marks]
e)	We had to wake up the hotel manager who was extremely grumpy and who hadn't even got the room ready for us. To cap it all there was no hot water. [2 marks]
f)	Things did not improve the next morning as the breakfast was quite inadequate. We were only offered coffee and stale bread. [2 marks]
g)	We were not very happy with the hotel which was much too far from a rather dirty beach. There was only one restaurant near enough for us to have lunch. [2 marks]
h)	The final straw was the very hot weather which was unbearable as the hotel rooms lacked air-conditioning and we were plagued by mosquitoes. [2 marks]

Practice Test 2

i) It was a quite dreadful holiday so I require a full explanation and our money back as soon as possible. [2 marks]

Yours faithfully,

[Total: 16 marks]

Paper 4 Listening (45 minutes)

Section A [One mark for each correct answer]

Picture 1 | × |
Picture 2 | × |
Picture 3 | 2 |
Picture 4 | 3 |
Picture 5 | × |
Picture 6 | 1 |

[Total: 6 marks (blank boxes receive 0)]

Section B [One mark for each correct answer]

7. central lounge
8. video displays
9. forty
   tax-free
10. free catalogue
11. sound-proofed
    air-conditioned
12. ground floor
    shower rooms
13. directly
14. subway
15. 15 minutes
    8.00/eight
16. yellow
    railway station

[Total: 15 marks]

Section C [One mark for each correct answer]

17. A   18. D   19. C   20. C   21. A

[Total: 5 marks]

Section D [One mark for each correct answer]

Task 1:   22. B   23. D   24. C   25. G   26. E
Task 2:   27. F   28. B   29. E   30. H   31. A

[Total: 10 marks]

Transcript

You have been given a question paper for the Certificate in Advanced English, Test Two. There are four parts to this test, Sections A, B, C and D, and you will hear each part twice, except for Section B which will be heard once only. There will be pauses to allow you to look through the questions before each part, and other pauses to let you think about your answers. At the end of every pause you will hear this sound.

tone

The tape will now be stopped while you look at your question paper. You must ask any questions now, as you will not be allowed to speak during the test.

[*pause*]

Section A. *You will hear a news item in which an accident involving a young girl is described. Look at the pictures and decide which ones show what actually happened. Some of the pictures are not correct. The first time you listen, put a cross against any pictures which are not correct. The second time you listen, put the correct pictures in the right order by putting 1 against the first picture you hear, 2 against the second picture, etc. Listen carefully. You will hear the piece twice.*

[*pause*]

tone

A young girl turned herself into a human torch after accidentally setting fire to her clothing in a park near the city centre. Thirteen-year-old Claudia Vianello from Italy was burned on her legs and stomach after a match set fire to her dress yesterday. She had been playing with a box of matches found in the park. Two friends, Gilbert Le Menton and Françoise Camel saved her from more serious injury by quickly beating out the flames. Firemen, on standby at the nearby Fire Station, hosed the girl down before an ambulance took her to the local hospital, where her condition was described as stable. Claudia, who expects to be in hospital for several days, said: 'I found the box with just two matches inside. I struck one and threw it down – I thought it had gone out. Then my legs became hot and I saw my skirt was on fire. It all happened so quickly.'

[*pause*]

tone

Now you will hear the piece again. [*The recording is repeated.*]

[*pause*]

Practice Test 2

That is the end of Section A.

[*pause*]

Section B. You will hear an information announcement about facilities offered at Schipol Airport in Amsterdam. Look at the sentences numbered 7–16 and complete them by writing one or two words in the spaces. Listen carefully as you will hear this piece once only.

[*pause*]

tone

If you do not already have a boarding card for your onward flight, be sure to go directly to one of the transfer desks. Most of the airlines are handled by the handling companies KLM and Aero Ground-services (each responsible for the handling of some 40 airlines). Their main transfer desks are situated in the central lounge.

[*pause*]

Before going to your gate, check the departure information on your boarding card against the most up-to-date information on the video displays (placed throughout the terminal) for possible gate changes. This is especially important for passengers who have already received their boarding card at the airport of origin.

[*pause*]

Schipol is perhaps best known for its award-winning tax-free shopping centre, with more than 40 shops offering a total of 100,000 items, including many designer originals. And Schipol's prices are among the lowest anywhere. A free catalogue is available in all the shops.

[*pause*]

The airport's sound-proofed and air-conditioned conference rooms (with optional catering) can accommodate up to 22 people. For reservations call (020) 601 23 89.

[*pause*]

Additional facilities on the ground floor include shower rooms and a nursery. In the event of a medical problem or emergency contact the ground staff or proceed to the first-aid station in Pier A.

[*pause*]

The railway station is situated directly opposite the terminal building. You can reach the station through the subway.

[*pause*]

Trains to Amsterdam Central Station depart every 15 minutes. Return fare 8 Dutch Guilders (approximately 4 US dollars).

[*pause*]

Yellow 'Centraal Nederland' buses to numerous destinations in Holland depart from in front of the railway station.

[*pause*]

tone

That is the end of Section B.

Practice Test 2

[*pause*]

Section C. You'll hear an interview between a manager and a member of her staff. Answer questions 17–21 by ticking the best answer A, B, C or D. You will hear the interview twice.

[*pause*]

tone

Natalie: Well, Dorothy, here are the schedules for next year, for what they are worth. (*sigh*)
Dorothy: Oh, thank you, Natalie, that'll really make the job a lot easier. Ah – but have you put target dates for each of your objectives?
Natalie: Well, that's quite impossible.
Dorothy: Why? I'm only asking for *target* dates. If you don't meet them, feel unable to meet them at a later stage, then you can reconsider them, change them . . .
Natalie: What's the point? Anyway, who needs these objectives, what are these objectives, who are they for . . . him, our director?
Dorothy: I need them – not just for our department but for the whole company. I think they will make things clearer for everyone, help people know where they're going, aiming at . . . Now come and sit down . . .
Natalie: I haven't time, there isn't enough time ever! Anyway, what I'm trying to say is that there's much more to the job then simply making a list of how and when we produce the products. In fact, that's the easy part and I just don't think it's helped at all. You mustn't forget the other side – that's just as important.
Dorothy: What do you mean exactly?
Natalie: The liaising with the other departments, the administrative back-up support. All this takes time.
Dorothy: I hope I'm not forgetting all that. Of course it's important, but we have to start somewhere. The product, our products, are the easiest thing to get hold of, they're tangible.
Natalie: Yes, but that's just it. They hide what the job's really about.
Dorothy: And that is?
Natalie: That's seeing people, talking to the people who buy our stuff. That's what gives people job satisfaction. That's what's really important.
Dorothy: Of course, I agree with you, but there's got to be an objective in doing all that, hasn't there?
Natalie: Oh, all this jargon, this management language. Where does it get us? All I know is that I am not doing what I should be doing, what I'm trained to do.
Dorothy: Or what you want to do? Your job is basically to produce a quality product. One that everyone wants and one that satisfies them.
Natalie: Oh, here we go 'product'. That's just words, words . . .
Dorothy: Perhaps we should meet again later and discuss things in more detail. Could you think about how you see your job now and how you see it developing . . .
Natalie: Developing! Disintegrating, more like. But, yes, all right. I think we should. I think you need to know about things, how I feel, what I have to do . . .
Dorothy: Monday, then, about two.
Natalie: Well, all right, but I may have other things to do.
Dorothy: I'll put it in my diary, then.

[*pause*]

tone

Practice Test 2

Now you will hear the piece again. [The recording is repeated.]

[*pause*]

That is the end of Section C.

[*pause*]

Section D. In a few moments you will hear various people talking. There are five extracts which are not related in any way except that everyone is talking about experiences they have had. Task One lists the topics that the people are talking about and Task Two lists the people. It is better to concentrate on Task One during the first hearing and Task Two during the second hearing. For Task One look at the topics labelled A–H. As you listen, decide in what order you hear them and complete the boxes 22–26 with the appropriate letter. For Task Two look at the people labelled A–H and put them in the order in which you hear them by completing the boxes 27–31 with the appropriate letter. Listen carefully. You will hear the people twice.

[*pause*]

tone

Man in wheelchair:
I think what I find most disheartening is people's reaction when they see me. They seem to think that if a person is in a wheelchair that they're only half-human or like a child or something. We don't get treated in the same way as the able-bodied, we don't come in for the same respect.

Long lost relative:
Getting a letter like that, out of the blue, was wonderful. I had given up hope of ever seeing my sister again.

Blind woman:
I remember when I lost my sight all those years ago, I said I'd never forget what my husband looked like. But you know, I have! (*with a laugh*) He feels very good looking though!

Nurse:
To go up there and be part of all that suffering was what I'd wanted. My medical training has been mainly in highly technical hospital environments, and so I couldn't help very much. But I'm still glad I went . . . Life seems sweeter somehow.

Proud parent:
She never talked much as a child, very self-composed you know. It's hard to see where she got the talent from, but there's no doubt she has a way with words. She's working on her second at the moment. She works all night sometimes. We're delighted, you know . . .

[*pause*]

tone

Now you will hear the piece again. [The recording is repeated.]

[*pause*]

That is the end of Section D. There will now be a pause to allow you to check your work.

[*pause*]

That is the end of the test.

Practice Test 2

Paper 5 Speaking   (15 minutes)

Note: In the examination, there will be both an assessor and an interlocutor in the room. The following notes use plural forms where appropriate, although we realise that a teacher may often be working alone for practice sessions.

You will need to refer to Paper 5 of Practice Test 2 in the Student's Book and the colour section 'Visual materials for Paper 5' also in the Student's Book.

Phase A   (approximately three minutes)

Interlocutor or assessor:
*Good morning. My name is . . . and this is my colleague . . .
And your names are?
First of all we'd like to know a little about you. Do you know each other?*

If yes:
*So perhaps you (Candidate A) could tell us about (Candidate B). Where's s/he from? What does s/he do? What are his/her hobbies? And (Candidate B), would you like to tell us about (Candidate A) now, please?
How long have you known each other?
What do you know about each other's country?*

If no:
*Could you please find out about each other? Talk about where you're from, what you do, what you're interested in, and so on.
Is there any special reason why you're studying English?
What plans do you have for your future?*

The questions in Phase A may be varied considerably according to the context, but will always cover introductions and general social conversation, following approximately the structure set out above.

Phase B   (three or four minutes)

1 STREET SCENES (Select one from many)

Int: *In this part of the test I'm going to give you some pictures to look at. Please look at page C4.*

Make sure that both candidates are looking at the STREET SCENES, pictures **2A–2D**.

Indicate one picture to Candidate A, ensuring that Candidate B does not know which one it is.

[To Candidate A] *I'd like you to describe your picture to (Candidate B). You have about a minute to do this.*

Practice Test 2

[To Candidate B] *I'd like you to listen and decide which picture is being described. If you are still uncertain when (Candidate A) has finished, you may ask him/her some questions to help you identify the picture. Otherwise, say briefly what helped you decide.*

APPROXIMATELY ONE MINUTE FOR THE DESCRIPTION

2 THE OFFICE (Compare and contrast)

Now I'm going to give each of you a picture to look at. Please do not show your pictures to each other. (Candidate A) I'd like you to look at picture 2E.

Show picture 2E to Candidate A.

Now, (Candidate B), will you look at picture 2F?

[To Candidate B] *I'd like you to describe your picture to (Candidate A), who has a picture which is similar to yours but not the same. Please describe it fully, and after about a minute I'll ask (Candidate A) to say how far his/her picture is different from and the same as yours.*

[To Candidate A] *Here's some spare paper in case you want to make any notes. All right?*

So, (Candidate B) would you start please?

APPROXIMATELY ONE MINUTE FOR THE DESCRIPTION

Thank you. Now, (Candidate A), I'd like you to tell (Candidate B) briefly how your picture is different from and the same as his/hers.

APPROXIMATELY 20 SECONDS

Now, would you like to compare the pictures?

ALLOW A FEW SECONDS, THEN PASS TO PHASE C

Phase C (approximately four minutes)

TRAVELLING COMPANION (Qualities in order of importance)

Indicate the list of 'Qualities in a travelling companion' (p. 53 in Student's Book) to both candidates.

Here is a list of qualities which you might value in a travelling companion. Imagine that you plan to spend a year travelling round the world. Together,

I'd like you to discuss these qualities and try to agree on their order of importance. You must reach agreement or 'agree to differ'. After four minutes you must report your decision.

APPROXIMATELY FOUR MINUTES FOR DISCUSSION

Phase D   (approximately four minutes)

*Which did you decide was most important? Why?
How far did you agree?
What did you disagree about? Why?
Would you like to spend a year travelling round the world? Why/why not?
What effect might it have on your career/on your personal development?
Is it best to travel when you're young, or is it something to save for retirement?
etc.*

Practice Test 3

Paper 1   Reading   (1 hour)

First text: 1. F   2. H   3. G   4. G   5. I   6. D   7. E
8. D   9. B   10. H   11. F   12. A   13. B   14. I

Second text: 15. B   16. D   17. D   18. C   19. D

Third text: 20. I   21. C   22. B   23. F   24. A   25. J
26. E   27. G   28. H

Fourth text: 29. D   30. C   31. B   32. A   33. C   34. C
35. D

Paper 2   Writing   (2 hours)

See pages 9–15 for assessment criteria and sample answers.

Paper 3   English in Use   (1 hour 30 minutes)

Section A

Question 1   [One mark for each correct answer]
1. C   2. C   3. B   4. D   5. D   6. B   7. C   8. A
9. B   10. D   11. C   12. B   13. B   14. C   15. D

Question 2   [One mark for each correct answer]
1. on   2. now/really   3. making   4. something   5. the/away
6. to   7. off/away   8. people/they   9. there   10. while/when
11. from   12. up   13. been   14. never/cannot   15. even

Section B

Question 3   [One mark for each correct answer]
1. museum   2. ✓   3. symbol   4. engineering   5. off   6. too
7. urged   8. grudgingly   9. trial   10. immediate   11. whole
12. ✓   13. literal   14. bewilderingly   15. ✓   16. their   17. ✓

Question 4 [One mark for each correct answer]

1. modern language   2. led/attended/addressed   3. opening/first
4. approaches   5. be replacing / replace   6. to attend / to come
7. followed by   8. the latest/newest   9. focus on / concentrate / consist of
10. giving talks   11. will end/close   12. should we/teachers
13. two places

Section C

Question 5 [One mark for each correct answer]

1. H   2. M   3. N   4. I   5. E   6. J   7. B   8. O
9. D   10. G   11. L

Question 6

Here is a sample answer:

a)	It was Friday evening and I was driving home about 6 o'clock.
b)	The traffic was heavy and it was getting dark when I joined a line of stationary cars on Victoria Avenue. [2 marks]
c)	There was obviously some hold-up ahead, probably caused by the traffic lights which seemed to be stuck on red. [2 marks]
d)	Suddenly I heard and felt a loud bang at the back of the car and it was pushed forwards as well as upwards. [2 marks]
e)	I was very shocked and I turned round and saw the driver of the car behind getting out of his car. [2 marks]
f)	His first words were 'I'm sorry, are you all right?' Then he explained his foot had slipped off the brake. [2 marks]
g)	My car was a mess. The bonnet had hit the car in front and had dented it seriously. [2 marks]
h)	The car behind had pushed the boot of my car right in. [2 marks]
i)	There was nothing I could do but sit and wait for the police as none of us could move. [2 marks]

[Total: 16 marks]

Practice Test 3

Paper 4 Listening (45 minutes)

Section A   [One mark for each correct answer]

1. ☒   2. ☑   3. ☒   4. ☑
5. ☒   6. ☑   7. ☒   8. ☒

[Total: 8 marks (blank boxes receive 0)]

Section B   [One mark for each correct answer]

9. students' hostel
10. history department/dept
11. tennis court(s)
12. fence
13. telephone (box)
14. library
15. (small) lake
16. restaurant
17. car park / lecturers' parking
18. engineering department/dept

[Total: 10 marks]

Section C   [One mark for each correct answer]

19. C   20. A   21. B   22. A   23. C   24. D

[Total: 5 marks]

Section D   [One mark for each correct answer]

Task 1:   25. F   26. A   27. B   28. E   29. C
Task 2:   30. C   31. H   32. F   33. E   34. B

[Total: 10 marks]

Transcript

You have been given a question paper for the Certificate in Advanced English, Test Three. There are four parts to this test, Sections A, B, C and D, and you will hear each part twice, except for Section B, which will be heard once only. There will be pauses to allow you to look through the questions before each part, and other pauses to let you think about your answers. At the end of every pause you will hear this sound.

tone

The tape will now be stopped while you look at your question paper. You must ask any questions now, as you will not be allowed to speak during the test.

[pause]

Practice Test 3

Section A. You will hear someone giving advice on creating a wildlife garden which will encourage wild animals and birds to visit. For questions 1–8 tick those pictures which show what you should do and put a cross against those which are not mentioned or are not suggested. Listen carefully. You will hear the piece twice.

[*pause*]

tone

Encouraging wildlife to visit your garden is both rewarding and surprisingly easy. Any garden, be it large or small, can become a haven for a wide range of plants and animals. This doesn't mean tearing up the lawn and abandoning the plot to wilderness. A wildlife garden should be colourful and attractive, pleasing both to the gardener and the nature-lover in us. The first step is to plan how the garden will take shape. This need not entail radical change. With a little modification, many existing features can be incorporated into the design – flower beds, lawns, rockeries, pools and hedges. To avoid disturbance, land set aside for fruit and vegetable plots and children's play areas should be spaced away from the wildlife garden if possible. Initially it's best to aim for a large variety, both in the types of habitat provided and the plant species introduced. Remember that it is important to provide food and cover for wildlife all through the year if you want to attract residents rather than mere visitors. A mix of habitats simulates meadowland, woodland edges and wetland. By its second summer we might expect this miniature reserve to yield an array of meadow flowers and woodland herbs. Butterflies and bees should be attracted to the blooms, and the pond is likely to be full of water creatures. As the garden matures, an increasing variety of birds and mammals may make use of the food supply and the plant cover. To help shy creatures before the new vegetation has developed, it is often a good idea to allow one section of the garden to become overgrown. Ideally this could be tucked away out of sight where it will not spoil the garden's visual impression. Never take plants from the wild to stock your garden. All plants that you might need for a wildlife garden are now available in seed packets or in pots from garden centres. However, it is important to select native species from stocklists, especially those which you know grow locally in the countryside. These are the plants alongside which our animal life has evolved and has a natural association with. Even if you have a very small garden there is a great deal that you can do to attract wildlife into it. A corner patch or some large plant pots seeded with a mixture of wild flowers can be visited by a variety of insects, wherever your house is located. Bird tables and nest boxes take up little space but can provide hours of birdwatching delight. You may not have room for a full woodland edge habitat, but try letting a hedge grow more freely and plant woodland flowers beneath it. You may be surprised at the wildlife that turns up.

[*pause*]

tone

Now you will hear the piece again. [*The recording is repeated.*]

[*pause*]

That is the end of Section A.

[*pause*]

Section B. You will hear someone explaining how to get to the English Language faculty on a university campus. On the map, complete the labels 9–18 showing various places and objects which he mentions. Listen carefully as you will hear this piece once only.

Practice Test 3

[*pause*]

tone

Now we're here outside the student's hostel and to get to the English faculty is very easy really, but there are a few dead-ends. If you go straight up here past the history department on your left, and don't turn down there on the left because you'll just hit the tennis courts. There's a fence either side. You can see the faculty from there but you can't get to it. So go on past it, and past the telephone box as well which is on the corner near the library. Continue down this road and you'll know you're OK because you'll come to a small lake with ducks on, usually. Now this is where you must turn left. Go round the lake and up the road on the left past the restaurant. So that's the third turning on the left from where we are now. Now, with the restaurant on your left, follow the road round to the left and you'll see the English faculty opposite. Mind you, don't try and get to it down the first road. That's just for the lecturers to park their cars, and there's a fence at the end too. No, go on going up the road and take the next right. And there you are, right opposite the engineering department – the English faculty. You shouldn't have any trouble at all. Just remember the phone box and the lake before you turn. OK?

[*pause*]

tone

That is the end of Section B.

[*pause*]

Section C. Listen to Richard Ramsay talking about how he invented and marketed a case for skis. Look at questions 19–24 and tick the best answer A, B, C or D. You will hear the interview twice.

[*pause*]

tone

Voice-over: Anyone who has ever gone skiing knows that carrying skis anywhere, especially around airports, is hell on earth. They are heavy, cumbersome, long, sharp and dangerous. The initial idea was to conquer the hassle of air travel but then it became apparent that some sort of easy-to-carry ski case would be equally valuable on the buses and coaches skiers use to get to and from the slopes. Skis are expensive items and need protecting. A skitube seemed such a practical, simple and obvious idea. It also made good business sense since over six million skis are sold every year worldwide with Europe accounting for 60 per cent of that figure. Ramsay began drawing up designs on the kitchen table in his Clapham flat.

Ramsay: I kept modifying and re-modifying. The case had to be easy to carry and able to hold every conceivable sort of binding and every ski length from as little as 160 cms up to 223 cms. The fact that the snow brakes on all skis would spring up inside the tube, making the whole more secure, and holding the skis in place, helped a great deal.

Voice-over: Eventually he overcame the problem with an extendable handle bridging all possible balance points. Then he began cold-moulding prototypes using a tough, light, impact-resistant polythene substance recommended to him by ICI as being able to withstand temperatures up to 40°C. The advice on what material his brainchild should be made of

	to 40°C. The advice on what material his brainchild should be made of cost him the price of a phone call.
Ramsay:	If you get on the phone you can speak, theoretically anyway, to anyone and find out a lot of quite exciting and very useful things – if you ask the right questions. People will willingly offer you advice for free, especially if they think they might be able to supply raw materials or get in on the action at some stage.
Voice-over:	Moulders were then approached to see if they were capable of actually making the tube. It was all cloak and dagger stuff.
Ramsay:	The idea was my only asset. I never showed anyone the whole thing at any one time. I just showed them parts. When you think you have a good idea you become paranoiac about not letting anyone else have it.
Voice-over:	Selling his car to fund overheads, Ramsay committed himself full-time to developing the marketing potential of his product. Having settled on a prototype, the problem of patenting arose.
Ramsay:	It is a fairly frightening business. If you don't pay for a patent you leave yourself wide open for some big company with greater resources to come in, steal the idea and market it harder than you. If you do decide on a patent, you have to come up with a great deal of money.
Voice-over:	In September 1988 the Skitube was officially patented, funded by a firm of venture capitalists. Some small businessmen tend to baulk at hands-on venture capital funding but Ramsay is realistic.
Ramsay:	It's very much like a marriage. You have to get on with them personally on a one-to-one basis because your success is very much tied up with theirs. There is a large element of trust involved but it is vital to retain the major share in the company. The problems faced by a lot of small businesses with potentially viable commercial products is that they cannot attract financial support and, if they do, lack resources and managerial skills to develop and exploit gaps in the market.
Voice-over:	Language has become the single biggest stumbling block so far for Skitube.
Ramsay:	It's very difficult indeed to carry on in-depth business discussions with someone who doesn't speak or understand English very well, and, vice versa, with German and French. We've found that although all the agents speak good English, the main decision-makers in European companies don't. You therefore have to rely on translators, interpreters and third parties to convince and persuade them that your product is worth buying. You have to let someone else do your sales spiel.
Voice-over:	Because of the simple economic fact that the UK forms only one per cent of the world ski market, Skitube must export and therefore must use European intermediaries. Ramsay is planning to teach himself German and has earmarked the other three members of staff for lessons in other languages.

[*pause*]

tone

Now you will hear the piece again. [The recording is repeated.]

[*pause*]

That is the end of Section C.

[*pause*]

Practice Test 3

Section D. In a few moments you will hear various people talking. There are five extracts which are not related in any way except that everyone is talking about being young. Task One lists the topics that the people are talking about and Task Two lists the people. It is better to concentrate on Task One during the first hearing and Task Two during the second hearing. For Task One look at the topics labelled A–H. As you listen, decide in what order you hear them and complete the boxes 25–29 with the appropriate letter. For Task Two look at the people labelled A–H and put them in the order in which you hear them by completing the boxes 30–34 with the appropriate letter. Listen carefully. You will hear the people twice.

[pause]

tone

A teenager:
It's not a good time, really. There are too many things to worry about – exams, girlfriends and so on – at least that's what bothers me at the moment.

An old lady:
I like to look at the young people today. They look so dressed up with their coloured clothes and fancy hair does. We couldn't do that when I was young – my mother only let me wear my best dress on a Sunday.

A parent:
We've found it a great strain having children. When they were babies they never seemed to sleep enough and now that they're teenagers it's difficult to get them out of bed!

An advertising consultant:
Our product is designed to appeal to young people so we've paid great attention to its design, its colour even. It has style and that's what they're after, you know. We're very sensitive about price, too. Low, but not too low – we want to get to those with a bit of money to spend.

Policeman:
There's been a lot of bother this year down by the river. Of course, it's left to us to sort it out when the kids get into trouble. If you ask me, it's the parents' fault – lack of guidance and very little control – that's the reason, you know.

[pause]

tone

Now you will hear the piece again. [The recording is repeated.]

[pause]

That is the end of Section D. There will now be a pause to allow you to check your work.

[pause]

That is the end of the test.

Paper 5   Speaking   (15 minutes)

Note: In the examination, there will be both an assessor and an interlocutor in the room. The following notes use plural forms where appropriate, although we realise that a teacher may often be working alone for practice sessions.

Practice Test 3

You will need to refer to Paper 5 of Practice Test 3 in the Student's Book and the colour section 'Visual materials for Paper 5' also in the Student's Book.

Phase A (approximately three minutes)

Interlocutor or assessor:
*Good morning. My name is . . . and this is my colleague . . .
And your names are?
First of all we'd like to know a little about you. Do you know each other?*

If yes:
*So perhaps you (Candidate A) could tell us about (Candidate B).
Where's s/he from? What does s/he do? What are his/her hobbies?
And (Candidate B), would you like to tell us about (Candidate A) now, please?
How long have you known each other?
What do you know about each other's country?*

If no:
*Could you please find out about each other? Talk about where you're from, what you do, what you're interested in, and so on.
Is there any special reason why you're studying English?
What plans do you have for your future?*

The questions in Phase A may be varied considerably according to the context, but will always cover introductions and general social conversation, following approximately the structure set out above.

Phase B (three or four minutes)

1 VILLAGE PLAN (Compare and contrast)

Int: *In this part of the test I'm going to give each of you a plan to look at. Please do not show your plans to each other. (Candidate A) I'd like you to look at plan 3A.*

Show plan **3A** to Candidate A.

Now, (Candidate B), will you look at plan 3B?

[To Candidate A] *You have a plan of a village, with various features marked and labelled. (Candidate B) has a plan of the same village but with many of the features missing. I'd like you to describe the village to (Candidate B) so that s/he can complete his/her plan. You have about a minute to do this.*

[To Candidate B] *I'd like you to listen and mark your plan as (Candidate A) describes it. Here is a pencil for you to use.*

APPROXIMATELY ONE MINUTE FOR THE DESCRIPTION

Now, would you like to compare your plans?

Practice Test 3

ALLOW A FEW SECONDS, THEN PASS TO PHASE B2

2 | EXHIBITION (Select one from many) |

Now I'm going to ask you to look at some pictures. Please look at page C7.

Make sure that both candidates are looking at EXHIBITION pictures 3C–3F.

Indicate one picture to Candidate B, ensuring that Candidate A does not know which one it is.

[To Candidate B] I'd like you to describe this picture to (Candidate A). You have about a minute to do this.

[To Candidate A] I'd like you to listen and decide which picture is being described. If you are still uncertain when (Candidate B) has finished, you may ask him/her some questions to help you identify the picture. Otherwise, say briefly what helped you decide.

APPROXIMATELY ONE MINUTE FOR THE DESCRIPTION

Phase C   (approximately four minutes)

| PROGRESS? |

Indicate the list of topics (p. 77 in Student's Book) to both candidates.

Here is a list of three topics. I'd like you to discuss whether they have, on the whole, improved or deteriorated over the past fifty years. You may talk about one or two places in particular, or about the world in general. You must reach agreement or 'agree to differ'. After four minutes you must report your conclusions.

APPROXIMATELY FOUR MINUTES FOR DISCUSSION

Phase D   (approximately four minutes)

What did you feel had improved? In what respect?
How far did you agree about this?
What did you disagree about? Why?
Which did you think had deteriorated? Why is that?
What would you like to see done about it?
Whose responsibility should it be?
Are there any other aspects of life which need urgent reform?
Which are they?
Do you both feel the same about this?
etc.

Practice Test 4

Paper 1 Reading (1 hour)

First text: 1. B   2. H   3. C   4. F   5. D   6. G   7. B
8. F   9. C   10. G   11. D   12. D   13. A   14. A
15. F   16. D   17. C

Second text: 18. A   19. B   20. D   21. C   22. B   23. A

Third text: 24. A   25. B   26. C   27. D   28. A   29. B
30. C

Fourth text: 31. B   32. E   33. A   34. D   35. B   36. A
37. C   38. D

Paper 2 Writing (2 hours)

See pages 9–15 for assessment criteria and sample answers.

Paper 3 English in Use (1 hour 30 minutes)

Section A

Question 1   [One mark for each correct answer]
1. C   2. B   3. D   4. A   5. B   6. A   7. D   8. A
9. B   10. C   11. B   12. C   13. A   14. B   15. A

Question 2   [One mark for each correct answer]
1. all   2. which/that   3. just/merely/only   4. it/but   5. least
6. became/got   7. nearly/just/only/almost   8. as   9. in/from
10. women's/new   11. for/on   12. what   13. jumping
14. over/around/round   15. being

Section B

Question 3   [One mark for each correct answer]
1. off   2. ✓   3. to   4. ✓   5. more   6. ✓   7. ✓   8. of
9. ✓   10. may   11. ✓   12. ✓   13. in/almost   14. ✓

Practice Test 4

Question 4 [One mark for each correct answer]

1. contend / put up   2. improvement   3. proceeds   4. our attention
5. vacancy/place   6. ask/invite   7. serving   8. the imbalance / the discrepancy   9. from   10. preferable/better   11. take up / fill
12. brought/offered / could bring /donate/give   13. leave them
14. edible/perishable goods   15. helping / offering assistance

Section C

Question 5 [One mark for each correct answer]

1. L   2. F   3. J   4. A   5. K   6. H   7. C   8. N
9. P   10. E   11. B

Question 6

Here is a sample answer:

> Dear Thomas
>
> It was wonderful to hear from you again.
>
> a) If you want to work in London why not look for something in the centre and come and share my flat? [2 marks]
>
> b) There are plenty of restaurants around here which often advertise for staff. I've noticed experience isn't always necessary. [1+2 marks]
>
> c) Last week I noticed that *Abigail's* in the High Street was looking for an assistant chef to work lunch times or evenings. The pay is low. I think you only get about £3 or £4 per hour. [2+1 mark]
>
> d) Do you know if it's necessary to have a work permit? I think you should check on that now and then I could arrange an interview for you next week, if you like? [1+2 marks]
>
> e) If you could send me your personal details, including any relevant experience and a couple of references, I could get started on the job application. [2 marks]
>
> f) Anyway, contact me soon as it's my birthday next week and we could have a party or go to the theatre. [2 marks]
>
> Best wishes,

[Total: 15 marks]

Paper 4   Listening   (45 minutes)

Section A   [One mark for each correct answer]

1. ✓   2. ☐   3. ☐   4. ✓
5. ✓   6. ☐   7. ☐   8. ✓

[Total: 8 marks]

Section B   [One mark for each correct answer]

9. cheaper/faster/quicker
10. overnight
11. reclining seats
12. public holidays
13. men shouting
14. sunny side
15. bottled water
16. lemon cologne
17. stop frequently / often stop (must have the whole concept)

[Total: 9 marks]

Section C   [One mark for each correct answer]

18. B   19. A   20. C   21. D   22. C

[Total: 5 marks]

Section D   [One mark for each correct answer]

Task 1:   23. D   24. C   25. E   26. F   27. B
Task 2:   28. D   29. C   30. B   31. A   32. G

[Total: 10 marks]

Transcript

You have been given a question paper for the Certificate in Advanced English, Test Four. There are four parts to this test, Sections A, B, C and D, and you will hear each part twice, except for Section B, which will be heard once only. There will be pauses to allow you to look through the questions before each part, and other pauses to let you think about your answers. At the end of every pause you will hear this sound.

tone

The tape will now be stopped while you look at your question paper. You must ask any questions now, as you will not be allowed to speak during the test.

[pause]

Practice Test 4

Section A. You will hear a recorded message welcoming new staff to the campus and giving them information about the services offered. For questions 1–8 tick those pictures which show you what you should do to receive the appropriate services or to help you keep to the regulations. Listen carefully. You will hear the piece twice.

[*pause*]

tone

Welcome to the university. We hope that you will soon settle in but, in order to help you with some of the basic practicalities, we have recorded the following information for you.

Repairs and maintenance
Any problems with housing should be reported to the Administrative Officer or a secretary in the School of English Language. Problems with plumbing and electricity will be dealt with, usually within 48 hours, but during the semester it may take longer. If you leave a spare key with the Administrative Officer then the work can be done while you are out.

Drinking water
Drinking water is distributed on Tuesday mornings. Leave your empty water container and 750 lire outside your flat. It is a good idea to put any change you collect aside for this purpose. If you are in your flat at the time, the man may well agree for you to pay the following week.

Rubbish
Rubbish should be placed in the yellow metal drums in front of the flats. Make sure that the lids are replaced securely for hygiene reasons.

Post
This will be delivered to the mail boxes or to your flat between eleven and twelve every day. Parcels will have to be collected from the faculty building.

Washing lines
You are asked not to hang laundry (and rugs, etc.) out on the balconies. Obviously this is to stop the place looking like a bazaar. We have found that a low washing line is not visible from the road. A folding low clothes line is even better.

Visitors
Security on the campus is tight. If you are accompanying your visitor by bus, taxi or car you should show your own identity card and explain that the person is your guest. When guests or visitors arrive unaccompanied on campus, the procedure is as follows: the security guard will inform the resident concerned, by phone, of the guest's arrival, and then the guest will be allowed to enter.

[*pause*]

tone

Now you will hear the piece again. [The recording is repeated.]

[*pause*]

That is the end of Section A.

[*pause*]

Practice Test 4

Section B. You will hear someone giving information about how to travel around Turkey. Look at the sentences 9–17 and complete them by writing one or two words in the spaces. Listen carefully as you will hear this piece once only.

[*pause*]

tone

Turkish State railways (TCDD) has a rail network 5,127 miles long. However, for the most part the trains are old and slow; buses are much faster and much more convenient, and cost less. Ankara, however, has a good rail service to both Istanbul and Izmir. There are a number of services during the day and an overnight service to both cities. Some services have couchettes and a dining car. Alternatively the Blue Train has very comfortable reclining seats. The fare on both these trains is very reasonable. Advance reservation is recommended, particularly during Turkish public holidays when the whole of Turkey seems on the move.

Unlike the trains, the coach companies in Turkey are all privately owned and are extremely competitive. If you walk into the bus station you will be surrounded by hundreds of men shouting the destinations of the coaches. These men are not ticket touts, but acting on behalf of the different companies, and they will take you to the ticket booth of their coach company. You will probably find a coach leaving within the hour, even for destinations some distance away. It is wise, however, to plan your journey in advance and book a seat. Check with the different companies whether you are planning in advance or not, so that you get the most convenient departure time. Otherwise you may find that you have reserved a seat on a bus departing in two hours while another company has a bus departing in 20 minutes. Seats are numbered, but you can ask for a particular seat. During the summer, plan to be on the shady side if possible.

Unfortunately there are no non-smoking areas, and the atmosphere may become very smokey. All services are efficient and cheap, but comfort varies. Everyone will tell you that the best service is Varan; it is also relatively more expensive. Pamukkale and Ulosoy are also good. All coaches carry bottled water in a refrigerated container, which is free on request, and at regular intervals you will be asked if you want some lemon cologne with which to refresh yourself. Stops are frequent along the journey during the day or night, so don't expect to get a good night's sleep.

[*pause*]

tone

That is the end of Section B.

[*pause*]

Section C. You will hear an interview with Gerda Geddes, who teaches the Chinese art of movement called 'Tai Chi'. Look at questions 18–22 and tick the best answer, A, B, C or D. You will hear the interview twice.

[*pause*]

tone

Presenter: With the absorbed, fluid grace of a dancer and the delicacy of a crane, Gerda Geddes glides through a sequence incorporating a series of swift, fighting kicks from the Long Yang form of 'Tai Chi' she has been practising for the past 40 years. Affectionately known as Pytt, Gerda Geddes was born in Norway but spent many years in China before bringing the art form to this country.

Practice Test 4

Gerda: It was very hot outside Shanghai in the summer, so for exercise my husband and I often went for walks in the paddy fields at dawn. The soil around Shanghai is very fertile; the fields are surrounded by drainage canals and are very flat, but when they grow gawliang (cattle fodder), which looks like very tall maize, the landscape becomes secretive and mysterious, and the canals are hidden. On one of these hot, misty mornings in 1949, as we turned a corner, we saw an old Chinese man, a farmer, standing by the water. Beside him, in a gilded cage, was a mynah bird. The old man was moving very slowly, performing incredibly beautiful, dance-like movements reflected in the water. He was so absorbed that he paid not the slightest attention to us. We just stood there mesmerised and I had the sensation of some strange force creeping up and down my spine. Later, I saw it in a park in Shanghai, but then came Mao and the Communists, and the Chinese suddenly became removed from the rest of us. But the more I thought about it, the more I realised this was what I'd always been looking for. Something rang a bell deep inside me, but at that time it was impossible to find a teacher because no-one could be seen with a Westerner.

Presenter: Moving to Hong Kong, Geddes persuaded a university lecturer enthusiast to pass on the secrets of this elusive martial art. Following tradition, he found her a master, a man of 74 called Choy Hawk Ping. Via the Chinese method of rote learning, she learned 'Tai Chi', for an hour a day, every day for two years, by copying.

Gerda: We communicated by him saying, 'Missee, you look see my body, you stand behind. Be like monkey. Copy me, use ears, listen my breathing, listen my hear.' When he died, his son, Choy Kam Man, took over. He moved like an angel. It was as if he didn't have a single joint in his body. He just flew, floated through everything.

Presenter: Originally undergoing a rigorous, four-year dance training in Norway and Sweden, she discovered that 'Tai Chi' brought an entirely different set of muscles into play.

Gerda: Trying to forget everything I'd ever learnt beforehand was essential. For me, it's always been this interest in what makes people tick – not so much the words they use, but the hows and whys of moving and acting. There's always this close connection between the psyche and the body, and that's where I feel the greatest growth potential of 'Tai Chi' lies. If you practise 'Tai Chi' daily as I do, it becomes part of your life. You become aware that your body changes and you have to acknowledge that ageing process. This realisation is very subtle. As the physical animal energy declines, it's somehow compensated for by the clarity of your spiritual energy. It can be hard acknowledging limitations, but through them you get in touch with something else. I'm sure that's the ultimate meaning of the 'Tai Chi': how do I grow old and still be friends with my body.

Presenter: After suffering a severe skiing accident and being told she'd never regain strength in the injured leg, Geddes used 'Tai Chi' to cure herself by regenerating lost muscle, and doctors often refer to her classes patients suffering from sore backs. 'Tai Chi' puts the legs in the right alignment and helps build up muscle strength – and vitality. From the Chinese point of view, the ageing process comes down to stimulating the flow of the 'Chi', keeping your entire circulation of energy going, so nothing in the body goes stale, using long oxygenating breaths.

[*pause*]

tone

Now you will hear the piece again. [*The recording is repeated.*]

[*pause*]

That is the end of Section C.

[*pause*]

Section D. *In a few moments you will hear various people talking. There are five extracts which are not related in any way except that everyone is talking about tourism. Task One lists the people who speak on the tape and Task Two lists what they are talking about. It is better to concentrate on Task One during the first hearing and Task Two during the second hearing. For Task One look at the people labelled A–H. As you listen, decide in what order you hear each person speak and complete the boxes 23–27 with the appropriate letter. For Task Two look at the topics labelled A–H and put them in the order in which you hear them by completing the boxes 28–32 with the appropriate letter. Listen carefully. You will hear the people twice.*

[*pause*]

tone

Greek hotelier:
I think it's unfair that the government has decided to stop further development. After all, what else is there to do on this island except provide for the tourists?

Woman:
We love it here. We come year after year just to feel the peace and enjoy the wonderful scenery. You can't beat Scotland for that. But I wouldn't want to live here all the time.

City-dweller:
Well, of course I know we need the tourists but I do wish they were more spread out during the year. In summer, you know, I avoid going to the town centre, it's so crowded.

Tour guide:
I suppose what I like about being a courier is the people; working with people and giving them a good time. It's hard work but basically it's being with people who want to enjoy themselves. That can't be bad, can it?

Conservationist:
On the whole I think tourism has done more harm than good to this region. Although it's brought money, in actual fact this money is not being used to keep the countryside maintained. We get 100,000 tourists every year, and I'm sorry to say, it looks like it.

[*pause*]

tone

Now you will hear the piece again. [*The recording is repeated.*]

[*pause*]

That is the end of Section D. There will now be a pause to allow you to check your work.

[*pause*]

That is the end of the test.

Practice Test 4

Paper 5 Speaking (15 minutes)

Note: In the examination, there will be both an assessor and an interlocutor in the room. The following notes use plural forms where appropriate, although we realise that a teacher may often be working alone for practice sessions.

You will need to refer to Paper 5 of Practice Test 4 in the Student's Book and the colour section 'Visual materials for Paper 5' also in the Student's Book.

Phase A (approximately three minutes)

Interlocutor or assessor:
> Good morning. My name is . . . and this is my colleague . . .
> And your names are?
> First of all we'd like to know a little about you. Do you know each other?

If yes:
> So perhaps you (Candidate A) could tell us about (Candidate B).
> Where's s/he from? What does s/he do? What are his/her hobbies?
> And (Candidate B), would you like to tell us about (Candidate A) now, please?
> How long have you known each other?
> What do you know about each other's country?

If no:
> Could you please find out about each other? Talk about where you're from, what you do, what you're interested in, and so on.
> Is there any special reason why you're studying English?
> What plans do you have for your future?

The questions in Phase A may be varied considerably according to the context, but will always cover introductions and general social conversation, following approximately the structure set out above.

Phase B (three or four minutes)

1 | BURGLARY SCENE (Compare and contrast) |

Int: *In this part of the test I'm going to give each of you a picture to look at. Please do not show your pictures to each other. (Candidate A) I'd like you to look at picture **4A**.*

Show picture **4A** to Candidate A.

> Now, (Candidate B), will you look at picture **4B**?

> [To Candidate A] I'd like you to describe your picture to (Candidate B) who has a picture which is similar to yours but not the same. Please describe it fully, and after about a minute I'll ask (Candidate B) to say how far his/her picture is different from and the same as yours.

[To Candidate B] *Here's some spare paper in case you want to make any notes. All right?*

So (Candidate A), would you start please?

APPROXIMATELY ONE MINUTE

Thank you. Now, (Candidate B), I'd like you to tell (Candidate A) briefly how your picture is different from and the same as his/hers.

APPROXIMATELY 20 SECONDS

ALLOW A FEW SECONDS, THEN PASS TO PHASE B2

2 | PEOPLE (Select one from many)

In this part of the test I'm going to give you some pictures to look at. Please look at page C8.

Make sure that both candidates are looking at PEOPLE pictures **4C–4N**.

Indicate one picture to Candidate B, ensuring that Candidate A does not know which one it is.

[To Candidate B] *I'd like you to describe this picture to (Candidate A). You have about a minute to do this.*

[To Candidate A] *I'd like you to listen and decide which picture is being described. If you are still uncertain when (Candidate B) has finished, you may ask him/her some questions to help you identify the picture. Otherwise, say briefly what helped you decide.*

APPROXIMATELY ONE MINUTE FOR THE DESCRIPTION

Phase C   (approximately four minutes)

| COMMITTEE BUDGETS |

Indicate the list of suggestions (p. 102 in Student's Book) to both candidates.

There is a list of suggestions as to how your education institution or company welfare fund should spend their budget. Together, I'd like you to discuss these suggestions and try to agree how you would spend the money. Give reasons for your choice. You must reach agreement or 'agree to differ'. After four minutes you must report your decision.

APPROXIMATELY FOUR MINUTES FOR DISCUSSION

Practice Test 4

Phase D   (approximately four minutes)

What did you decide was most important?
Why?
How far did you agree?
What did you disagree about? Why?
In what ways is it important for employers to look after their staff by providing good facilities?
etc.